Kama Sutra

The Total History of The Ancient Kama Sutra and Modern Uses of the Love Book

Charlotte Brown

Charlotte Brown

paraphrase any part or the content within this book without the consent of the author or copyright owner. Legal action will be pursued if this is breached.

Disclaimer Notice:

Please note the information contained within this document is for educational and entertainment purposes only. Every attempt has been made to provide accurate, up to date and reliable complete information. No warranties of any kind are expressed or implied. Readers acknowledge that the author is not engaging in the rendering of legal, financial, medical or professional advice.

By reading this document, the reader agrees that under no circumstances are we responsible for any losses, direct or indirect, which are incurred as a result of the use of information contained within this document, including, but not limited to, —errors, omissions, or inaccuracies.

Table Of Contents

Charlotte Brown

Introduction

The *Kama Sutra*, written by Mallanaga Vatsyayana, is an ancient Hindu text that examines relationships between men and women, and the different types of connections that men and women may form. Contrary to popular belief, the *Kama Sutra* is not a sex manual, nor did it originally contain illustrations of sexual positions. While one part of the *Kama Sutra* does address sexual positions and sexual acts, this is far from the primary purpose of the text.

Topics addressed in the *Kama Sutra* include the way in which a man and woman should conduct themselves properly in society, during courtship, in a marriage, and within the context of a sexual relationship. The author, Vatsyayana, examines relationships of a purely sexual nature, loving romantic relationships, and marriages involving multiple wives, all of which were an acceptable and normal part of the ancient Hindu culture about which

Vatsyayana was writing. After all of the advice and guidelines are provided, Vatsyayana ends the *Kama Sutra* with a discussion of how an individual can attract a lover by magical and occult means if none of the other methods work, and also sets out magical options for increasing one's sexual ability where there is a presence of performance issues.

This book will examine the history and philosophy behind the *Kama Sutra*, and will discuss the contents of the *Kama Sutra* and the various lessons that were provided by the text. The *Kama Sutra* is a fascinating study: not only does it provide a clear understanding of ancient Indian and Hindu culture; but it also demonstrates that while there are some vast differences between that ancient culture and modern day society, there are also far more similarities than one might expect.

The book also talks about various translations that have been done of the *Kama Sutra*, and how the text has impacted modern culture.

After you have read this book, you will have a much more thorough understanding of the *Kama Sutra*, not only regarding its content but also of how well it reflects the culture that it discusses and how it has impacted modern-day culture.

Charlotte Brown

Chapter 1
Underlying Philosophy and the Writing of the *Kama Sutra*

The *Kama Sutra* is an Indian Hindu text composed by Mallanaga Vatsyayana sometime between the first century CE and the sixth century CE. It is not known exactly when it was written, although references both within the work and to the work in later texts indicate a possible range. In the *Kama Sutra*, when Vatsyayana is discussing the dangers of sexual attraction and emotion and how sexuality needs to be kept in moderation. He uses as an example of an incident where the king, Satakarnia Satavahana, killed his wife Malayevati by striking her during the heat of passion. Based on available evidence, it appears that Satavahana lived during the first century CE, so Vatsyayana must have lived during or after that time. At the other end of the range, the writer Virahamihira refers to Vatsyayana in his writings, and Virahamihira lived during the sixth century CE.

The *Kama Sutra* is part of a collection of ancient religious texts from India called the *Kama Shastra* (meaning the discipline of Kama, who was the Hindu god of love). It was intended primarily for the upper castes of the Hindu culture.

The *Kama Sutra* is so named because it discusses "Kama," one of the four goals of a Hindu life. "Kama" means "desire," which includes but is not limited to sexual desire. "Sutra" is a metaphorical line or thread that connects things. The *Kama Sutra* addresses the various parts of life, including romantic and sexual relationships, and how they connect to each other and the four goals of a Hindu life.

In addition to Kama, the other four goals of life (the Purusharthas) are Dharma, which is virtuous living; Artha, which represents (material) prosperity; and Moksha, which is the freedom or liberation from the cycle of birth, death, and rebirth. Artha, Dharma, and Kama are goals for everyday life while Moksha comes into play at the end of one's life when one is approaching death, and will be entered into the death and rebirth cycle.

In the ancient Hindu culture, Dharma was considered a "higher goal" than Artha, with Artha being higher than Kama. However, there were two exceptions to this approach: the king was expected to focus on Artha because that is how the people would prosper and public women (courtesans) were to focus on Kama. Aside from the two exceptions (kings and courtesans), the overall principle is that, if there is a conflict between two of the principles, then the 'higher goal' wins. So if doing something to earn money would not be virtuous, then a person must choose the virtuous option, even if it means losing some material wealth.

Pleasure (Kama) was considered to be the least important of the goals. It was recognized that the senses could be dangerous and could lead people to temptation, which would cause them to disregard the first and second goals of Dharma and Artha.

According to the *Kama Sutra*, and other writings on which it was based, during childhood, the focus should be on learning how to make money so that one can support himself and his family later in life. Then, during youth and middle age, the focus should be on pleasure (as this is when reproduction happens, which requires pleasure). Finally, in old age, the focus should be on Dharma, or living virtuously. The overall principle remains that, aside from the exceptions mentioned above, Dharma is overall a higher goal than Artha, which is overall a higher goal than Kama.

The basic premise of the *Kama Sutra* is that to achieve a happy marriage, it is essential that men and women are educated in the complexities of relationships and the arts of pleasure, both sexual and intellectual. The text sets out the basic guidelines that govern physical and sexual relationships, love, and marriage, in accordance with Hindu culture and law.

The *Kama Sutra* is very notable for an ancient text in that it focuses on the bringing of pleasure to women, and warns that if a man is not successful in this enterprise, then she may, fully-justified, seek her pleasure elsewhere. The *Kama Sutra* and its principles and guidelines were taught to young women as part of their education before entering into marriage. Men were also taught these principles and were expected to live by the rules and guidelines set out in the text.

Origin Stories

There are several origin stories associated with the creation of the *Kama Sutra*. The first is that Nandi, the sacred bull, and doorkeeper of the Indian God Shiva, bestowed the *Kama Sutra* upon humankind. He heard the god Shiva with his wife, Parvati, during a sexual encounter, and was so inspired by what he heard that he spoke about it to others. That utterance was eventually recorded and passed on to humans in the hopes that it would assist them with procreation and maintaining healthy relationships.

The second origin story is that Prajapati, an Indian deity (god of creation), created 10,000 chapters, Shiva gathered the chapters together, and Shvetaketu (Sage Uddalaka's son and a teacher of philosophy) reduced the knowledge into 500 chapters. Vatsyayana, who was seen by some as a saint, played the role of transcribing the chapters into Sanskrit.

Writing of the Kama Sutra

In the preface to *Kama Sutra*, Vatsyayana references both origin stories and discusses the seven parts of the original script from the gods. He then discusses how the original script was handed down from the gods and expounded upon by various other writers before Vatsyayana.

He cited the works of these other authors who had previously created the works from which he drew information. Essentially, the seven parts of the *Kama Sutra* were an abridgment of the works by (in order): Dattaka; Suvarnanabha; Ghotakamukha; Gonardiya; Gonikaputra; Charayana; and Kuchumara.

The seven parts are as follows:

- Sadharana (general topics) by Charayana;
- Samprayogika (embraces, etc.) by Subarnanabha;
- Kanya Samprayuktaka (the union of men and women) by Ghotakamukha;
- Bharyadhikarika (about one's own wife) by Gonardiya;
- Paradika (about the wives of other people) by Gonikaputra;

- Vaisika (about courtesans) by Dattaka. Dattaka wrote about courtesans upon receiving a request from the "public women" (courtesans) of Pataliputra. Also known as Patna, Pataliputra was the capital of the Magadha Empire during the last few centuries BCE, under several empires including Haryanka, Nanda, Mauryan, Shunga, Gupta, and Pala. It was the center of learning and the arts for the Hindu culture; and

- Aupamishadika (the arts of seduction, medicines, etc.) by Kuchumara.

Contrary to popular belief, the *Kama Sutra* is not a book about tantric sex, nor does it discuss sexual rites that are dealt with in some forms of Tantric practice. Nor is it a sex manual, although it does involve some inspection of sexual acts. In fact, sexual acts are a small portion of the content of the *Kama Sutra*. The focus is more on relationships and marriage, the differences between the behavior of men and women, and how men and women can attract and relate to each other. There is also an examination of courtesan practices which will be helpful to the larger population. In the last part of the text, the *Kama Sutra* deals with magical ways of causing one to be attracted to you or being aroused if you are unable to achieve it through the means discussed in the previous sections of the text.

Differences Between Ancient and Modern Cultures

What makes the *Kama Sutra* of particular interest to people in today's society is that it demonstrates an ancient society that was open to the ideas and issues surrounding sexual relationships, that valued sex as a sacred and vital part of healthy life and happy relationships. The *Kama Sutra* discusses homosexuality, polygamy, and female sexual pleasure – topics which are relatively controversial in today's society, and yet which were discussed openly and comfortably in Hindu culture 2000 years ago.

Chapter 2
Part I – Introductory Remarks

This chapter deals with the introduction to the basic tenets of the *Kama Sutra* and the types of matters that will be discussed throughout the book. It sets the groundwork for the rest of the text. It addresses the three goals of Hindu life (Dharma, Artha, and Kama), talks about the 64 arts of love, and describes how a proper man conducts his life and his household. It also points out that certain women are unfit for relationships, and that friends and messengers play important roles in relationships.

On the Acquisition of Dharma, Artha, and Kama

Vatsyayana introduces the concepts of Dharma, Artha, and Kama, and relates that these principles should be followed and applied at different times during the life of a man, whose life period is said by Vatsyayana to be one hundred years. Childhood should be dedicated to Artha, learning the art of making money, so that one is equipped to support oneself and one's family later in life. Then, during one's youth and middle age, the focus should be on Kama as well as Artha as this is the time when relationships are made, and procreation takes place. Finally, a man should focus on Dharma in old age, with the eventual goal of achieving Moksha, or the release from the continuous cycle of birth, death, and rebirth.

Artha is defined by Vatsyayana as the acquiring of land, gold, arts, wealth, cattle, and friends. It is not only the acquisition, however, but it also requires that one protects and increases previously obtained properties. To learn Artha, a man could study and observe the king's officers and merchants.

Kama, or "desire," is the enjoyment of the world through the five senses, and involves the mind, the body, and the soul. The experience of pleasure that arises from the interaction between a sense organ and the object that it is sensing is called Kama. One was to learn Kama from the aphorisms of love that had been written about and discussed by previous Hindu scholars and religious men, as well as from the everyday lives of citizens who experienced Kama on a daily basis.

Dharma, as the highest goal, meant following the commands of the Shastra, the Holy Writ of the Hindus. It involves sacrifice and the avoidance of certain conduct which would harm the world, including the eating of meat. Dharma was to be learned from the Holy Writs and those who had studied and practiced them.

Vatsyayana noted that while three goals were to be focused on more during particular life stages, overall Dharma was the 'better' goal and should be observed in specific circumstances over Artha and Kama. There were exceptions to this rule: the King was to practice Artha over Dharma, because it was the responsibility of the king to ensure the prosperity of his people, and public women (courtesans) were to focus on Kama as that was essentially the purpose of their existence.

In this section, Vatsyayana not only discussed the three life goals or principles, but he also raised what he believed were four likely objections to the principles, and provided answers to those objections. For instance, he raised the possible objection that Kama was not the proper subject of a book, because it could be found everywhere and was practiced in some form, even by animals. Vatsyayana's answer to this was that a proper sexual relationship between a man and woman was necessary to the survival and maintenance of healthy relationships. Relationships in which only Kama was practiced were those of "brute creation" would be unhealthy and unlikely to survive. Vatsyana also says that Kama is an act that is dependent on the man and the woman involved in it. They (the man and woman) need to apply the proper means in order for the act to be more than just a practice of "'brute creation.'"

Another objection that might be raised is that making pleasure a goal is weak and that seeking only pleasure can lead to misfortune and misery. However, Vatsyayana counters this argument by pointing out that such a stance is hollow because food, sex, and other pleasures of the senses are vital to life and in fact, can be considered the consequences of following dharma and artha. He does caution that pleasure should not be sought in excess but should be instead sought with prudence and restraint. One cannot, however, ignore it or hold it in contempt because such an act would make one lose the most important forces in life.

On the Arts and Sciences to be Studied

This section is one that is often referenced by scholars of the *Kama Sutra,* as well as ancient Indian and Hindu cultures. Vatsyayana sets out the arts that a learned citizen should know and states that both men and women should learn these arts. In response to the potential objection that women who were not allowed to study science should also not be permitted to study the arts of love, Vatsyayana pointed out that women live and informally study the *Kama Sutra* every day, and that the learning of the arts for the purpose of applying them on a daily basis to relationships was not the same as learning a science for more academic purposes. He did note, however, that women should study either alone or with a "confidential friend," and recommended that this friend be one of a few options: the daughter of her nursemaid from childhood (only if that daughter was already married); a completely trustworthy female friend; her aunt; an old female servant; or her own sister.

The arts were divided into four types, which can loosely be described as creative abilities, analytical abilities, physical and practical abilities, and intellectual abilities. Creative abilities included specific arts such as singing, playing a musical instrument, decorating, making jewelry, magic or sorcery, and the very specific ability to "'play on musical glasses filled with water.'" Analytical abilities involved the art of imitation and reading, which included chanting and intoning. Physical and practical abilities encompassed the use of weapons, carpentry, knowledge about precious metals and gems, understanding of gardening, and the talent of teaching parrots to speak, as well as many others. Finally, the intellectual arts set out by Vatsyayana involved composing poetry, gambling, disguising one's appearance, mathematics, and the ability to determine a man's character from his features. The arts as described by Vatsyayana were certainly a curious mix of general abilities and very specific talents.

At the end of the section discussing the arts, Vatsyayana noted that courtesans who were beautiful had a good personality, and had studied the arts, would be awarded the distinction of Ganika, which meant "public woman of high quality." Such a courtesan would receive a seat of honor in any gathering of men, and would be respected by the king. For other women, the knowledge of these arts would allow them to become their husband's favorite, regardless of the number of other wives he had, and would also allow a woman to support herself if she was to become separated from her husband through death or other circumstances. As for men, these arts would enable them to quickly and easily gain the affection of women, and to please their wives.

The Life of a Citizen

In this section, Vatsyayana discussed how an average citizen, or "a man about town," should conduct his life and his household. Vatsyayana was very specific in many of his recommendations. He stated that a man should obtain a house in a city, large village, or some location where there were plenty of other good men around. The house should be close to water, and should have a garden, and one inner and one outer room. The inner room is for the women, and the outer room is for the men and women to inhabit together. In the outer room, there should be a bed covered with a clean white cloth and two pillows, one at the head of the bed, and one at the foot. There should be a stool by the bed where the "fragrant ointments" for use during sexual encounters would be placed, on the ground there should be a pot for spitting, and a lute should be hanging somewhere on a peg made from the tooth of an elephant. In the garden, a man was to set up a whirling swing and a common swing, as well as a parterre with flowers for sitting and enjoying the view.

In addition to how a house should be set up, Vatsyayana also described the personal hygiene habits that "the householder" should follow, including brushing his teeth in the morning, ornamenting his body, and looking in the glass to ensure that his appearance was satisfactory. He should bathe daily, cover his body in oil only every other day, shave his head and face every four days and the rest of his body every five or ten days (likely to avoid the gathering of lice). Three meals a day were to be eaten, in the morning, afternoon, and at night. After breakfast, the householder should spend some time teaching his parrots to speak (every house must have parrots in cages), and afterward, he must spend time cock and quail fighting. After a midday nap, lunch would be eaten, and then the householder should meet with his friends. In the evening, after supper, there would be singing, and then the man (and any friends with whom he had been singing) would go wait in his room for the women to come to and join him. The man and his friends would then be responsible for entertaining the woman with a "loving and agreeable conversation," presumably followed by a sexual encounter, if so desired.

Vatsyayana then went on to describe particular conduct that should be followed during social events, such as drinking parties, gardens or picnics, social events involving men and women, and festivals. Vatsyayana also set out a list of social activities that would be appropriate, including eating tender ears of corn, decorating each other with flowers, and going out on moonlit nights. These activities were only to be pursued by a man with a courtesan (not another type of woman), or by a courtesan with her servants or friends.

Finally, Vatsyayana discusses the different types of people, other than the "'man about town'"/average citizen and the courtesan. These types of people are appropriate to use as messengers between lovers and when requiring assistance during a lover's quarrel. A Pithamarda was a man who has no wealth and is unmarried, with limited possessions, but who is skilled in the arts, and so is received in the company of citizens and courtesans. A Vita was a man who had previously had wealth and was a householder, and is married, and so is honored by citizens and lives on means provided by citizens. And a Vidushaka (also known as a Vaihasaka) was essentially a jester, talented with the arts related to entertainment and held to be trustworthy.

As a summary of the ideas set out in this section, Vatsyayana placed one of the verses that he dispersed throughout the *Kama Sutra*: "'A citizen discoursing, not entirely in the Sanscrit language, nor wholly in the dialects of the country, on various topics in society, obtains great respect. The wise should not resort to a society disliked by the public, governed by no rules, and intent on the destruction of others. But a learned man living in a society which acts according to the wishes of the people, and which has pleasure for its only object is highly respected in this world.'"

About the Kinds of Women Resorted to by the Citizens, and of Friends and Messengers

For producing lawful progeny and the respect of one's peers, Vatsyayana wrote that a man of the four castes was expected to enter a lawful marriage with a woman of his own caste. Practicing Kama with women in a caste higher than one's own, or from one's own caste but who had been 'previously enjoyed' by others, was strictly forbidden. On the other hand, practicing Kama with women of lower castes, who had been banished from their own caste, who had been married twice, or who were courtesans, was not prohibited, as long as it was solely for the purpose of pleasure and not marriage. These women who were acceptable only for what were essentially sexual relationships were known as Nayikas.

Also, certain women were strictly prohibited to all men, including lepers, such as a woman who was either extremely white or extremely black, a near relation, and a woman who publicly expressed her desire for sex.

As for friends, Vatsyayana set out the types of friends who were to be trusted: a childhood friend; one bound by an obligation; one who is of similar personality and enjoys the same interests; a fellow student; one who knows all of your secrets, and whose secrets that you know; and the child of your nursemaid/nanny. Friends should possess certain qualities, including honesty, steadfastness, free from jealousy, and loyal.

Finally, Vatsyayana discusses messengers, i.e. people who can be used as go-betweens for lovers. Messengers should also possess certain qualities, including manners, business ingenuity, boldness, and reading body language.

The Kama Sutra, for all its mythic sexiness and supposed revelations about the power of intercourse, is remarkably didactic in its presentations. That said, it is a remarkably assured collection of wisdom and anecdotes, one that has achieved a legacy as the "greatest book of love ever written" (Anand 23). While certainly many of its conclusions and prescriptions are bizarre to say the least, the Kama Sutra is singular in its "'unabashed directness of the confrontation of sexual relations, the subtleties of apperceptions of feeling, mood, and emotion, the delicacy of nuances of love rendered by a mind, freed from all fears, inhibitions, and awkwardness of the accepting, routine society.'" Indeed, it is this frankness, this freedom from inhibition and awkwardness that should guide our analysis as we continue, so that we can understand how sex is placed in the context of self-realization, rather than as a prurient act in itself.

The book begins with a "salutation" to dharma, artha, and kama, the three forces that intertwine for self-realization. Dharma is the duty one has to fulfill over the course of one's lifetime in order to work off "karma," or the debts accumulated from selfish actions. Dharma is the most important part of being human, and as we get older, we must focus on it more and more in order to achieve "moksha," or liberation from the constant rebirths on Earth. Artha is the accumulation of material wealth, specifically those things that help one rise in status, but also applies to the elements that ensure a comfortable life. Early on, we are more conscious of artha as we seek to make a living, but we ultimately lose focus on artha as we grow older. Finally, kama is the experience that comes with the pleasure of the senses. Kama is the first thing we focus on when we are young, but we gradually lose interest in kama as we focus on artha, and then dharma.

The Kama Sutra was collected by Vatsyayana, and each of the seven sections of the book is purportedly elaborated upon by an ancient sage. This first book, General Principles, has a number of strategies for addressing the reader, but the first one we encounter is the Challenge-Response method, not unlike the Socratic method. Upon stating that dharma is more important than artha, which is in turn more important than kama, the author ensures that the reader doesn't translate this into a casual treatment of the Kama Sutra. Thus he uses challenge-responses to not only establish the necessity of kama - for it is, after all, the source of life itself - but also to underscore its value as a source of pleasure, or bodily satisfaction. Humans are driven to seek out food and sex, implies the author - so why should we judge this desire? It is our duty, our nature, to learn to enjoy it as best we can.

The prescriptions for women may strike modern readers as sexist, but in a way Vatsyayana is attempting to decode the mystery of femininity. He is less concerned with a woman's role in sex, and focuses more on her role in the household. He suggests that a woman should develop intellectual, physical, and even athletic pastimes to show off her powers and skills. Hidden between the lines of all these prescriptions is a remarkable respect for women - the opposite of the attitude found in a number of other religious or ancient texts. What's outlined, then, is a comprehensive set of arts, practices and behaviors that will "complement" the Kama Sutra and enable a woman to be the best lover, wife, and mother she can possibly be.

Vatsyayana ended this section with a verse about friends: "'The man who is ingenious and wise, who is accompanied by a friend, and who knows the intentions of others, as also the proper time and place for doing everything, can gain over, very easily, even a woman who is very hard to be obtained.'"

What Vatsyayana suggests here is that love is not only an art, but a science - something that requires careful courtship, psychology, and even a go-between. This sholka is in itself subtly urgent, as it implies that a man can only become wise and ingenious by studying and assimilating all that will unfold in the pages that follow.

Charlotte Brown

Chapter 3
Part II – On Sexual Union

This Part of the *Kama Sutra* is the one that is most commonly referenced in today's culture, as it is the one that deals specifically with sexual acts. However, even within this section, the sexual act is not the sole focus. It also deals with the matching of individuals on a physical basis to determine the appropriateness of a sexual connection, as well as the different types of love that can be found between people.

Kinds of Sexual Union According to Dimensions, Force of Desire or Passion, Time Kind of Union

In this section, Vatsyayana talks about the three classes of men, which men are divided into based on the size of their sexual organs. The classes are the hare, the bull, and the horse. Women also are divided into classes, depending on the depth of their sexual organs: the deer; the mare; or the elephant.

Within these classes, the equal unions are the hare and the deer, the bull and the mare, and the horse and the elephant. While unequal unions were certainly not prohibited, according to the *Kama Sutra* they would not be optimal pairings to lead to the best possible sexual encounter.

Individuals were also classed into categories of desire: small; middling; and intense. While Vatsyayana does not discuss the optimal connections between these classes, one can assume being at opposite ends of the spectrum would make for a less than optimal sexual encounter.

The final classification set out by Vatsyayana in this section relates to the amount of time that an individual spends during a sexual encounter. Again there are three options: short-timed; moderate-timed; and long-timed. Vatsyayana does note that this categorization is perhaps less important when it comes to females, as males are completely spent once they are done, while females are not necessarily so, and could continue if their male partner was longer-timed than they were.

Vatsyayana then enters into a fairly extensive discussion of the difference between male and female pleasure. He notes that some may say that women enjoy less pleasure than men because of the different workings of their bodies, but Vatsyayana essentially argues that women and men can have different biological functions (particularly concerning procreation), while still equally enjoying pleasure from a sexual encounter.

Vatsyayana goes on to note that when one takes into consideration the three types of categorizations (size of sexual organs, level of sexual desire, and time spent during sex), there can be multiple unions that would result in pleasure for both parties, even if that union within one particular category would not be optimal.

The section finishes with Vatsyayana discussing the various types of love that an individual might experience. There are four basic types of love: love acquired by continual habit; love resulting from the imagination; love resulting from belief; and love resulting from the perception of external objects.

Love from habit arises from the continual performance of an act, and can be applied to the love of sex, of hunting, drinking, etc. Today it might be considered as an addiction. This has become the basis for many scientists who argue that love is, simply put, a habit. This type of love is basically based on repetition – if you have sex with someone on a regular basis and spend a lot of time with that person love will eventually exist between you. This is because you know that in order for life and sex to be fulfilling, love must come to be. Since this form of love comes from practice, it may be something that can be consciously developed.

Love arising from imagination is based on something that an individual hopes will happen, but has not yet experienced or is not currently experiencing. In this kind of love, one imagines what love is supposed to be like. One gives it a definition and categorizes it and then seeks out someone who fits that definition and categorization. This type of love becomes a way by which one can control and direct one's feelings. It leads to a romance that can be cautious and, as a result, a little awkward. Vatsyayana also seems to believe that this type of love is the most ephemeral and doubtful. When imagination fades and reality takes its place, such love may not last.

Love resulting from belief refers to the mutual love between two people that has been demonstrated through caring actions. It can be a consequence of two people coming to the mutual decision that they are in love and looking to prove it through the aforementioned caring actions.

And finally, love resulting from the perception of external objects is essentially the enjoyment of aesthetics and sensations. This type of love is obvious to everyone except for the couple involved. In such a case, the couple is so deep into the love that they can't see it for what it is, but the world can see it. This type of love cannot be conceptualized, only experienced by us. According to Vatsyayana, the pleasure that arises from this type of love is superior to the pleasure from all other types of love.

Of the Embrace

In this section, Vatsyayana discusses the sexual acts as set out in the Kama Shastra. He notes that this teaching is also often referred to as 'Sixty-four' (Chatushshashti), and mentions that there is a great deal of argument over why it is referred to by this name. In the end, though, Vatsyayana posits that this name is merely accidental and has no specific meaning.

There are four types of embrace that occur between lovers but are not directly within the context of sexual intercourse: touching; rubbing; piercing; and pressing. These embraces are somewhat different than what one might think based on the names. The touching embrace and the piercing embrace are types of embraces that occur between people who are getting to know each other. The touching embrace means the initial hesitant touches when one first meets and is attempting to garner attention and determine if the other is interested. Vatsyayana uses the example of when a man uses some pretext to touch a woman's body with her own as a result of attraction. The piercing embrace is basically if a woman accidentally (whether a true accident or not) "pierces" a man with her breasts while, for example, bending down to do something, and in return the man grabs the woman's breasts.

The rubbing and pressing embraces, on the other hand, take place between lovers who are comfortable with each other. The rubbing embrace refers to the act of two lovers rubbing their bodies against each other, and the pressing embrace is when one lover presses the other lover's body forcibly against a wall in passion.

There are also four types of embraces that occur either at the start or during intercourse: twining of a creeper; climbing a tree; mixing sesame seed with rice; and milk and water. The twining of a creeper embrace, also known as Jataveshtitaka, is when a woman clings to a man as a creeper does to a tree, and twines herself around him seeking a kiss. The climbing of a tree (Vrikshadhirudhaka), also a kissing embrace, occurs when a woman climbs a man's body to obtain a kiss. These two embraces take place when the lovers are standing and are a precursor to the actual sexual intercourse.

Mixing of sesame seed with rice (Tila-Tandulaka) describes an embrace where two lovers are lying in bed and are encircling each other with their arms and thighs and rubbing against each other. The milk and water embrace (Kshiraniraka) is when a man and woman are so passionate about each other that they disregard pain, and embrace so tightly that they seem to be melding their bodies, usually with the woman sitting in a man's lap or laying on him in bed.

There are also four embraces relating to body parts: thighs; jaghana (navel to thighs); breasts; and forehead. The embrace of each involves one lover placing his or her own body part against that same body part of the other lover.

On Kissing

Vatsyayana starts this section by noting that while some people may believe that kissing and embracing is appropriate only before sexual intercourse, and striking and sounds is only appropriate during, Vatsyayana believes that any of the acts can take place in any order, as long as both individuals are enjoying the acts.

Vatsyayana states that there are certain places appropriate for kissing: forehead; eyes; cheeks; throat; bosom; breast; lips; and inside the mouth (French kissing). He acknowledges that the people of some countries will also kiss on the joints of the thighs, arms, and navel, but argues that he does not believe that this is appropriate for all people.

A variety of types of kisses are discussed in this section, including the straight kiss (when lovers' lips come together straight on), the bent kiss (lovers' heads are bent toward each other), the turned kiss (turning a lover's head toward you to get a kiss), and the pressed kiss (pressing the lower lip with more force). The "kiss that kindles love" is when a woman holds her lover's face while he sleeps and kisses him, and a "kiss that turns away" is when a woman kisses her lover when he is not paying attention to what she is doing. A reading of the *Kama Sutra* would seem to indicate that there is a type of kiss for most interactions between lovers.

Vatsyayana also discusses different intensities of kissing: moderate; contracted; pressed; and soft. The intensity that is appropriate varies depending on the part of the body that is being kissed.

Vatsyayana ends the section on kissing with a verse: "'Whatever things may be done by one of the lovers to the other, the same should be returned by the other, i.e. if the woman kisses him he should kiss her in return, if she strikes him he should also strike her in return.'"

On Pressing or Marking, or Scratching with the Nails

According to Vatsyayana's discussion of this topic, it would appear as though marking a lover with one's nails was a common occurrence, although he does note that it should only be practiced by lovers when it is enjoyed by both. In fact, Vatsyayana specifically notes that if a woman were seen by a strange man to have nail marks on her body, he would be filled with respect for her, while a man with nail marks on his body would be attractive to women.

Vatsyayana sets out a list of eight forms of marks that might be made: sounding; half-moon; circle; line; tiger's nail; peacock's foot; jump of a hare; and leaf of a blue lotus. A sounding mark is when the nails are pressed so lightly that no actual mark is left, and the only sign is that the hairs on the body are standing as a result of the touch. The sounding mark is made specifically on the chin, breasts, lower lip, or jaghana (navel to thighs).

A curved mark on the neck or breasts is called a half-moon. When half-moons are made opposite to each other, it is called a circle. This is usually made on the navel, the buttocks, and the thighs.

A line can be made on any part of the body. When the line is curved and marked specifically on the breast, it is called the tiger's nail. When all five nails are used to make a curved mark on the breast, this is called the peacock's foot. Vatsyayana notes that the peacock's foot requires a great deal of skill to be done properly, and so should be rewarded with praise.

When the five nails are used to make marks close to each other and the nipple, this is the jump of a hare. Finally, the leaf of a blue lotus is literally when a mark is made on the thigh or breast that resembles the leaf of the blue lotus.

Vatsyayana states that these are the more common types of marking and that there may be many others as there are innumerable levels of skill. He notes that variety is a necessity for love, and so the skill to make different types of marks is valuable, especially in courtesans.

Vatsyayana finishes the section by noting that there are verses that have been written about the practice of marking a lover with one's nails. "'The love of a woman who seeks the marks of nails on the private parts of her body, even though they are old and almost worn out, becomes again fresh and new. If there be now marks of nails to remind a person of the passages of love, then love is lessened in the same way as when no union takes place for a long time.'" This verse demonstrates what an important role the practice played in sexual encounters of that time.

On Biting, and the Means to be Employed with Regard to Women of Different Countries

Vatsyayana begins this section by noting that it is appropriate to bite anywhere where one can kiss, with the exception of the upper lip, the eyes, and the interior of the mouth. He also sets out the qualities of ideal teeth: bright; unbroken; sharp; and of proper proportion.

Vatsyayana then goes on to discuss the different types of bites that can be made on a lover's body. The hidden bite is one where redness of the skin is the only mark to show that a bite occurred, and there are no teeth lasting marks. A swollen bite is one where the skin is pressed down on both sides. A point bite is when two teeth are used to bite a small portion of the skin, and a "line of points" is when all of the teeth are used.

The "coral and the jewel" refers to the biting using one's lips and teeth, with the lips being the coral and the teeth being the jewels. When a bite is made with all of the teeth, it is called a line of jewels.

A broken cloud bite is one where marks of unequal depth are made in a circle and is made only on the breast. The biting of a boar refers to several rows of marks close to each other and is a sign of intense passion.

Each of these types of kisses is to be made only on certain parts of the body. The hidden, swollen, and point bites are to be made on the lower lip while the coral and the jewel and the swollen bite (again) are done on the cheek. Vatsyayana makes note that the "cheek" refers to the left cheek specifically. The line of points and line of jewels bites are to be made on the throat, the armpit, and the thigh joints, with the line of points also available to be impressed on the forehead and thighs.

Vatsyayana then goes on to discuss the biting habits of women from certain countries and the differences between them. Women of the central countries for example, between the Ganges and Jumna rivers, do not like marking with nails or biting while the women of Balhika enjoy striking. In all, Vatsyayana goes through 15 different areas and discusses the sexual practices of women from each. He does note, however, that just because women from one area generally like or dislike something, it does not necessarily mean that every woman from that area likes or dislikes it and that variations can occur.

Of the Different Ways of Lying Down, and Various Kinds of Congress

The best sexual position to be used by lovers will depend on the size of each lover's sexual organs. For example, when a deer woman (with a less deep yoni, or vagina) has sex with a bull or a horseman, she should lie in a way that will widen her yoni. On the other hand, an elephant woman who is having sex with a hare man should lie in a different type of position that will cause her yoni to contract.

A deer woman has three ways in which to lie down so as to increase the depth of her yoni. In the widely opened position, the woman will lower her head and raise her middle parts, allowing the man to enter her from behind. If she lies on her back, spreads her thighs, and keeps them wide apart, this is the yawning position. Finally, the position of Indrani, which requires practice, is when the deer woman lies on her back and spreads her thighs, with her legs bent so that they are doubled up. This position is best when the deer woman is having sex with a horseman.

There are many positions which can be used regardless of whether a woman is a deer, mare, or elephant, or the man is a hare, bull, or horse. The clasping position, for example, is when the lovers lie facing each other and have their legs straight against the other's legs. When the lovers start in the clasping position, and the woman presses her lover with her thighs, this is the pressing position.

A yawning position that can be used by all lovers and so is different than that for a deer woman with a bull or horseman is when a woman, lying on her back, raises both of her legs and places them on her lover's shoulders. Similarly, an alternative pressed position that can be used by anyone is when a woman lies on her back and bends her knees so that the bent legs are pressed between her and her lover's chest. This position can be altered by the woman stretching out one of her legs, which is then called the half-pressed position.

Vatsyayana also discusses the names of positions when more than two parties are involved. When a man has sex with two women, this is called a united congress. When he has sex with more than two women, it is called a congress of a herd of cows.

Vatsyayana finishes this section with a verse about the various kinds of congress: "'An ingenious person should multiply the kinds of congress after the fashion of the different kinds of beasts and birds. For these different kinds of congress, performed according to the usage of each country, and the liking of each individual, generate love, friendship, and respect in the hearts of women.'"

Of the Various Modes of Striking, and of the Sounds Appropriate to Them

This section starts with Vatsyayana explaining that sexual intercourse is similar to a lover's quarrel, concerning the passion that is involved, and because love tends to cause disputes. This section discusses the types of, and places for, striking during sexual intercourse for the purpose of the pleasure of both parties.

The places that are special for striking are the shoulders, head, space between the breasts, back, jaghana (navel to thighs), and side. These can be struck in only four ways: with the back of the hand; with the fingers a little contracted; with the fist; and with the open palm of the hand.

Vatsyayana then notes that, because striking causes pain, there are sounds of crying that are associated with the act of striking. There are eight distinct crying sounds that may be produced: Hin; thunder; cooing; weeping; Phut; Phat; Sut; and Plat. He also points out that there may be other sounds such as words that express sufficiency, prohibition, or pain or praise, and that a person may also make sounds that are similar to some animals, such as the pigeon, parrot, bee, flamingo, or quail.

Then follows a discussion about which blows should be used when depending on the stage and type of sexual act. For instance, when a woman is sitting on a man's lap, she should be struck on the back with the fist, and she should give similar blows in return to him while making cooing and weeping sounds. It is interesting that the sounds to be used are not only for the person being struck but may also be used by the person striking.

Vatsyayana does note that the people of the southern countries are prone to striking with instruments – including the wedge on the bosom, scissors on the head, a piercing instrument on the cheek, and pinchers on the breasts – but argues that this practice was barbarous and should not be picked up on by people from other locations. In fact, he feels so strongly about this that he sets out a few examples where the use of weapons went wrong. King

Satakani Satavahana accidentally killed his wife with a pair of scissors, and the king of the Panchalas accidentally killed a courtesan Madhavasena with a wedge, both during sexual intercourse.

He follows up this argument and ends the section with a verse about how sexual intercourse arouses such passion that anything can happen, and so lovers (especially men) should be very careful and pay attention to what they are doing, because all acts are not appropriate for all times or all people: "'Such passionate actions and amorous gesticulations or movements, which arise on the spur of the moment, and during sexual intercourse, cannot be defined, and are as irregular as dreams. A horse having once attained the fifth degree of motion goes on with blind speed, regardless of pits, ditches, and posts in his way, and in the same manner a loving pair become blind with passion in the heat of congress, and go on with great impetuosity, paying not the least regard to excess. For this reason, one who is well acquainted with the science of love, and knowing his own strength, as also the tenderness, impetuosity, and strength of the young women, should act accordingly. The various modes of enjoyment are not for all times or for all persons, but they should only be used at the proper time and in the proper countries and places."'

About Women Acting the Part of a Man, and of the Work of a Man

This section discusses what a woman must do when her male lover is tired from too much sex, for example, that she must take over the brunt of the sexual activity, which generally is the work of the man. This can happen either during sexual intercourse (congress) if a man tires, or from the beginning of congress if the man is too tired to start.

Vatsyayana then discusses what the general work of a man is during the act of congress. Essentially, it is the man's responsibility to undress the woman, coax her into the act if she is shy, and touch and caress her body in such a way that she is made comfortable and desirous. At all times, he should be taking note of what things are pleasing to the woman. A man can determine what a woman likes from certain signs from the woman: she relaxes her body; closes her eyes; and shows increased willingness for the act. On the other hand, if a woman shakes her hand, bites or kicks the man, or continues to move after the man has finished his part of the congress, this means that the man has failed to please the woman. Vatsyayana states that the man cannot leave things like this, and the man must rub the woman's yoni with his hand and fingers until she is pleased, at which point he should then have sex with her again.

There are certain actions that a man is to take during sexual congress. When the sexual organs are brought together directly, this is called "moving the organ forward." A man holding his lingam and turned it around in the yoni is called "churning." When a woman lowers her yoni, and the man strikes the upper part of it with his lingam it is called "piercing," but the same thing being done to the lower part of the yoni is called "rubbing." "Pressing" involves the yoni being pressed by the lingam for a long time. Removing the lingam from the yoni and then striking the yoni with the lingam is called "giving a blow." If a man rubs only one part of the yoni with the lingam, this is called the "blow of a boar," and rubbing both parts is called the "blow of a bull." Finally, if the man puts his lingam into the yoni and moves it up and down frequently, without taking it out, this is called the "sporting of a sparrow," and takes place at the end of sexual intercourse.

When a woman takes on the work of a man during congress, in addition to the nine moves discussed above, she also has three additional options: the pair of tongs, the top, and the swing. For "the pair of tongs," the woman holds the lingam in her yoni and keeps it there for a long time. When a woman, during congress, turns around like a wheel, this is called the "top." This move requires practice to do properly. If, during the "top" move, the man lifts up the middle part of his body and the woman turns her middle part around, this is called the "swing" and is also quite complex.

Vatsyayana finishes off the section about a man's work and a woman taking that over with a verse on the subject: "'Though a woman is reserved, and keeps her feelings concealed, yet when she gets on the top of a man, she then shows all her love and desire. A man should gather from the actions of the woman of what disposition she is, and in what way she likes to be enjoyed. A woman during her monthly courses, a woman who has been lately confined, and a fat woman should not be made to act the part of a man.'"

Of the Auparishtaka or Mouth Congress

According to Vatsyayana, oral sex ("mouth congress") was an act appropriate to be performed only by eunuchs, unchaste and wanton women, and servants and maids. A proper woman or man would not perform mouth congress, although both could receive it from one of the types of people who were permitted to perform it. Vatsyayana does not go into any detail about how mouth congress is to be performed on women.

Women were to receive mouth congress only from female eunuchs, who would live as courtesans and be available to women for this purpose. This was called "Auparishtaka." Male eunuchs would live as "shampooers" (those who are paid to bathe men), and during the act of shampooing a man, they could initiate the act. If a man demanded mouth congress, then the eunuch was to protest but eventually given in, but if a man did not ask for it, the eunuch could take the initiative and proceed with the act.

Unlike with mouth congress on women, Vatsyayana goes into fairly extensive detail about exactly how mouth congress is to be performed on a man by a eunuch. There are eight moves, to be done in a specific order. After each step, the eunuch should express his desire to stop, but will eventually continue.

First, the eunuch must perform the "nominal congress," which is where the eunuch holds the lingam in his hand and puts his mouth on it in various places. Then, the eunuch will cover the end of the lingam with his fingers and press the sides of the lingam with his lips and teeth, which is called "biting the sides." The next step is "outside pressing," which is to kiss the tip of the lingam in a closed mouth kiss. The eunuch then moves to "inside pressing," which is kissing the tip of the lingam and putting it into his mouth. The eunuch should then kiss the tip as though it were the lower lip of the mouth, which is called "kissing." The next step is to touch the lingam with the tongue, all over the lingam, and this is called "rubbing." The last two steps are "sucking a mango fruit," which involves putting half of the lingam into the eunuch's mouth and kissing and sucking it. This is followed by the last step, "swallowing up," which is where the eunuch puts the entire lingam into his mouth. This last act will finish the mouth congress.

Vatsyayana then discusses the practices of various peoples with respect to mouth congress. The people of Eastern

India, for example, do not deal with women who practice Auparishtaka (i.e. female eunuchs), while the people of Ahichhatra would deal them, but not for the purposes of mouth congress.

Although Vatsyayana begins this section with a discussion of who should and should not perform mouth congress, he ends it with a brief point that really, when it comes to sexual congress and love, each person should act according to the customs of their country, but also to their own inclinations. He follows this statement with a verse about the different possibilities that may arise: "'the male servants of some men carry on the mouth congress with their masters. It is also practiced by some citizens, who know each other well, among themselves. Some women of the harem, when they are amorous, do the acts of the mouth on the yonis of one another, and some men do the same thing with women. The way of doing this (i.e. of kissing the yoni) should be known from kissing the mouth. When a man and woman lie down in an inverted order, with the head of the one towards the feet of the other and carry on this congress, it is called the "congress of a crow."

Of the Way How to Begin and How to End the Congress.
Different Kinds of Congress and Love Quarrels

In this section, Vatsyayana describes how the pleasure room is to be set up, decorated with flowers and perfumes, and attended by servants. When the woman enters, after being bathed and dressed, she should be invited to drink refreshments. The man should sit the woman on his left side, hold her hair with his left hand, and embrace her with his right. The man and women should then carry on "amusing conversation," including talking about sexual matters. They might also sing or play musical instruments. Finally, when the woman is ready and filled with desire, the man should dismiss the servants and then proceed with sexual congress.

Once congress is finished, the lovers should go separately to the washing-room to clean themselves up. After returning to the pleasure room, they should eat some betel leaves, and the man should apply ointment to the woman's body. They should eat and drink, usually, foods that are sweet and soft. They may sit outside on the terrace and enjoy the moonlight. If this is done, Vatsyayana states specifically that the man should point out the different planets and stars to the woman.

As to the different kinds of congress, Vatsyayana states that there are seven types: loving congress, after a quarrel or journey or some separation; subsequent love, in the infancy of love; artificial love, when the lovers are attached to other people emotionally; transferred love, when the man is thinking of another woman; congress like eunuchs, which occurs with servants and is strictly for the purpose of sexual release; deceitful congress, between lovers from different areas; and spontaneous congress, which covers any other time that two regular lovers decide to engage in sexual intercourse.

Vatsyayana discusses love quarrels, but only addresses one possible cause: when a woman is angered because she hears the name of her rival or is called by her rival's name. If this occurs, the woman should, according to Vatsyayana, throw a temper tantrum, and the man must attempt to calm her. The woman is not to give in, and must go to the door of the room, but not leave. Eventually, she should allow her lover to appease her, and should embrace him while still admonishing him for his actions. If a woman is in her own house when a quarrel takes place, then she is permitted to leave, and should return once a messenger has worked to reconcile the two lovers. It would appear from Vatsyayana's discussion of a lover's quarrel that the woman is fully entitled to display her anger, and it is the man's responsibility to apologize and resolve the issue.

All in all, the man who knows the 64 "divisions" of the Kama Sutra will become a Nayaka (leader) anywhere he goes, since these divisions are looked upon with love by all women, and the love of women is the key to gaining respect in any society.

The Kama Sutra does have its contradictions. At the end of the first book, a Shloka suggests that a man who is wise, ingenious, and aware of the lessons of the Kama Sutra will find the woman he desires, no matter how unobtainable she initially seems. At the start of Book 2, however, we come to find a stringent set of instructions that divide men into three classes, depending on their phallus size, and women into three classes, based on the depth of their vagina. You might end up in an unequal (or impossible) union if you have sex with someone of the wrong class. In other words, a man with a large phallus (a "'horse'") can only sleep with a woman with an exceptionally deep vagina (a "female elephant"), or risk an unequal, or low, relationship. The Kama Sutra certainly doesn't forbid unequal relationships - indeed, the book rarely forbids anything - but it does suggest that matches based on anatomical similarities make for the best unions.

The matter of orgasms takes up quite a bit of Book 2, with the author trying to designate exactly how the two sexes should climax in relation to each other during intercourse. A man can climax easier and earlier than a woman, so foreplay is crucial for building up a woman's pleasure enough that there is the possibility of climax together at the end of intercourse. The author implies that it's quite easy for a male to achieve satisfaction. As soon as he orgasms, he's finished - his desire is sated no matter what. Yet a woman achieves satisfaction much more slowly and less completely, and so it's important for a man to pay special attention to ensuring her orgasm, or risk having an unequal sexual congress.

Oral sex is mentioned mainly in the context of the "Masseur." Neither a man nor a woman, these entities are incapable of achieving sexual satisfaction through any means other than oral sex, since their desires are kept mostly secret except in the case of their professional roles as masseurs. In this context, they can carefully coerce their subjects to allow them to perform oral sex. According to the Kama Sutra, the mouth can only be used by the "normal" male and female for nominal kissing, biting of the sides of the bodies, licking, swallowing, or even sucking a mango - all in service of foreplay.

Oral sex is also mentioned in the context of homosexual interactions - male servants who perform oral sex on their masters, women of the court who perform it on men or other women, and young masseurs who engage in mutual oral sex, known as the Kakila position, in which each participant's head aligns with his or her partner's genitals.

There is little to say about the 64 divisions of sexual congress, but we should note that all of these sexual instructions do fall into fairly rigid gender roles. Indeed, there is an entire section that delineates the strict rules under which a woman can take over the man's role and control the rhythm of intercourse. The Kama Sutra does allow for other forms of sexual union, including oral sex between men, oral sex between women, and even a "third gender" between man and woman who finds principal satisfaction as a masseuse and preys upon his subjects to achieve satisfaction through oral sex. This is a strange little diversion, but suggests that the Kama Sutra is determined to afford everyone the potential to achieve true pleasure (albeit in the context of a strict hierarchy).

Chapter 4

Part III – About The Acquisition of a Wife

In this part of the *Kama Sutra*, Vatsyayana discusses marriage arrangements, and how a citizen should go about acquiring a wife. He starts with a discussion of the importance of a proper marriage, in that it will lead to children, more friends, love, and the acquisition of Dharma and Artha.

According to the Holy Writ, a marriage involves the union of male to a female virgin of the same caste. Such a union results in the acquisition of dharma and artha, as well as the production of offspring, affinity, an increase in friends, and untarnished love. Moreover, a man should find a woman with a good family, whose parents are alive, and who is at least three years younger than himself. The author adds that if the woman is wealthy, well connected, has strong relationships with family and friends, and has good hair, teeth, breasts, and overall health, then the marriage will be even more auspicious. The man should possess all of these qualities as well.

To create a marriage with this virgin maid, the Kama Sutra encourages all manner of deceits and diversions. For instance, the friends of both families should extol the potential bride or groom to the other party's family, "even to exaggeration of all the excellencies, "in order to be more convincing. One of the male's friends "should disguise himself as an astrologer, and declare the future good fortune and wealth" of the couple, should they get married. However, there are a number of "types" of girls that should be avoided. These include a girl with an ill-sounding name, a girl who has been concealed in the house for bodily defects, a girl who is engaged to another, a girl with white spots on her body, a manly or heavily-built girl, a hunchback, and a balding girl.

For the first three days after marriage, the girl and her husband should sleep on the floor, abstain from sexual pleasure, and eat their food without seasoning. For the next seven days, they should bathe amidst the sounds of auspicious musical instruments, dine together, and pay attention to their relatives. On the night of the tenth day, the man should begin gentle love play, but mainly using soft words to inspire confidence in the girl. Sexual pleasure must not begin until the male has her trust - for women, "being of a tender nature, want tender beginnings." Once he slowly builds this confidence, he can then teach her the "64 arts," tell her how much he loves her, and then, having overcome her bashfulness, "begin to enjoy her in a way so as to delight her."

A poor man should have his own ways of trying to win over a girl. He should spend time with the girl and amuse her with various games and diversions. They should play games together, but more than anything, the man should show great kindness to the girl in order to show that he is fit to be trusted. The man should go out of his way to show he is different by giving her gifts of playthings, revealing his many talents, and impressing her with his prowess. Once he sees that she loves him, he is on his way to winning her family over, as well.

Once the girl begins to show her love through outwards signs and motions, her lover should hold her hand, embrace her, and even rub and press against her to gain some sort of sexual fidelity. Finally, he should express his feelings and make the girl realize his lovesickness, "for though a man loves a girl ever so much, he never succeeds in winning her without a great deal of talking." A girl should hold out physically at first, especially when a man demands sexual intercourse, but when a woman is certain that she is truly loved and is convinced that her lover is devoted to her and will not change his mind, then she can be persuaded to give herself up to him.

There are several forms of marriage. There is the marriage according to religious law, when a girl is won over and acts openly with a man as his wife. This is a marriage done in the presence of the ceremonial fire: the Gandharva form of marriage. When the girl cannot make up her mind or will not express her readiness to marry, then the man should use deceit to acquire her.

On Marriage

Due to the importance of marriage, it is necessary that a man makes the right choice when selecting his bride. She should be from a good and wealthy family, with parents still alive; she should be at least three years younger than him, and have many friends and family; she should be beautiful and have a good body, neither too thin nor too large. In no circumstances should a man marry a woman who has already had sex, and is therefore no longer a virgin (unless the man she has had sex with is her potential husband).

To arrange the marriage, the man's parents and other family members, as well as any friends as applicable, should make the girl's parents aware of the faults of other potential suitors and should extol the virtues of the man. It is recommended that one friend pretends to be an astrologer, and advise the girl and her family that they will receive good fortune if she marries the man. Another friend should make the girl's mother jealous by implying that he has better options available for a bride.

Vatsyayana states that marriage should only take place when the signs and omens are favorable and circumstances are right. If a girl is asleep, crying, or has left to avoid the marriage, then the marriage should not occur. A man should also avoid certain traits in a girl to be married, including if she has crooked thighs, a bald head, is formed like a male, is a younger sister, or has (hasn't?) fully arrived at puberty.

Once a girl becomes marriageable, her parents should make sure that she is dressed and adorned as prettily as possible, and display her at public events. She should go with female companions to various social events, such as weddings and sporting events so that she can be seen by potential suitors. Once a suitor has demonstrated his interest, the parents of the girl shall invite the man to bathe and dine, but the formal marriage arrangement shall not be made at that time.

Of Creating Confidence in the Girl

When a girl is first married, it is expected that she will be shy and nervous. Vatsyayana describes the ways in which a man can win his bride over so that she is not fearful or nervous of him. For the first three days after the wedding, the husband and wife should sleep on the floor, should not engage in any kind of sexual activity, and should eat unseasoned foods. For the seven days after that, they should bathe while surrounded by the sound of musical instruments, decorate themselves, eat together, and spend time with family. On the evening of the tenth day, the man should start to approach his bride with soft words and embraces, but should only do what she likes and should not force himself upon her.

Once the bride has accepted her husband's embrace, he should then urge her into a conversation with him, and should gradually increase the level of embraces. No actual sexual congress should take place on the tenth night. Each night after, the man should work to increase his wife's confidence in and comfort level with him more, until she eventually is ready for the act of sexual intercourse.

The strategy to be pursued by a new husband is summarized in the verse that Vatsyayana included at the end of this section: "A man acting according to the inclinations of a girl should try to gain her over so that she may love him and place her confidence in him. A man does not succeed either by implicitly following the inclination of a girl, or by wholly opposing her, and he should, therefore, adopt a middle course. He who knows how to make himself beloved by women, as well as to increase their honor and create confidence in them, this man becomes an object of their love. But he who neglects a girl, thinking she is too bashful, is despised by her as a beast ignorant of the working of the female mind. Moreover, a girl forcibly enjoyed by one who does not understand the hearts of girls becomes nervous, uneasy, and dejected, and suddenly begins to hate the man who has taken advantage of her; and then, when her love is not understood or returned, she sinks into despondency, and becomes either a hater of mankind altogether, or, hating her own man, she has recourse to other men."

On Courtship, and the Manifestation of the Feelings by Outward Signs and Deeds

In this section, Vatsyayana discusses how a man (or rather, a boy) should court a girl, and how a girl and boy should show their affection for and attraction to each other.

Often, a man will find the girl that he loves while he is still a boy. If this is the case, he should woo the girl by playing games that are suitable for their age, including making garlands of flowers, pretending to be family members, or playing with cards. He should choose activities that will please the girl that he is pursuing. They should also play games in a group so that she can see that he is trustworthy and that people like him.

In addition to wooing the girl, a man should also become friends with her nursemaid's daughter, who will be a friend of the girl and will pass on information to her. If he is kind to the nurse's daughter and shows her that he is knowledgeable in the ways of women and the arts of love, then she will talk to the girl and her parents about his excellent qualities.

A boy or man should also give a girl gifts to impress and attract her. The more unique a gift is, the more a girl will notice him. Options for gift ideas listed by Vatsyayana include dolls, cooking utensils, bird cages, ointments, and food. Whether the gift should be given in public or private depends on the circumstances, including the type of gift. By providing the girl with gifts, he shows that he understands what she likes and that he is willing and able to take care of her.

As for a girl, she will show her interest differently, according to Vatsyayana. A girl will not look a man directly in the face, but through her hair or from under her eyelids. She will be hesitant to speak with him, and will speak either in very limited amounts or through a female companion. She will, however, be unwilling to leave the place where he is, and will speak to her companions in a way that will capture his attention. She may also give a man, with one of her companions acting as a messenger, a token of affection such as a ring or garland of flowers.

In short, Vatsyayana posits that it is a man's job to pursue a potential bride while it is a girl's job to be pursued and to encourage attention only in a proper and ladylike manner.

About Things to be Done Only by the Man, and the Acquisition of the Girl Thereby.

Also What is to be Done by a Girl to Gain Over a Man, and Subject Him to Her

Once a girl starts to show her affection toward a man, as discussed above, then he should increase the level of courtship. When they are participating in games or attending social events, he should hold her hand, or practice the initial embraces (such as the touching embrace) discussed in Part II. He should always try to be near her and touching her, and should tell her about his feelings and his love for her. Vatsyayana also recommends that a man should pretend to be ill so that she will come to his house to see him and take care of him. When she begins to prepare his medicine, he should tell her that he would want only her to prepare the medicine and no other. This fake illness should last for three days, so that the man will have plenty of opportunities to see the girl privately and to talk with her, thereby increasing her comfort with him.

A girl can work to seek the attention of a man in whom she is interested, particularly if she has good qualities and is well-bred, but her family is not wealthy, or she is an orphan. In these cases, she will need to work harder than other girls to attract a good husband. She should go out in public with her companions so that he will notice her, give him gifts, and make it clear that she has learned the arts of life and the arts of love (although she should still be a virgin). A girl should never make the first overt gesture, however, because that will result in a loss of dignity. She should still require him to pursue her with respect to sexual encounters, and should only eventually give herself to him after he has committed to marrying her.

On Certain Forms of Marriage

This section seems to be somewhat contradictory to the previous ones, where Vatsyayana stated that marriage should not take place if the girl is unwilling. In this section,

Vatsyayana sets out various ways in which marriage might come about, including several circumstances where the girl has refused him or has not yet made up her mind about whom to marry.

In the situation where the man and woman have agreed that they will marry, the man will obtain fire from the house of a Brahmin, and will bring it to the girl's house. He should spread Kusha grass on the ground at her house, make an offering to the fire, and then the marriage ceremony can take place. This is called the Gandharva form of marriage.

Vatsyayana then proceeds to discuss various situations where the girl is perhaps not entirely willing to be married to the man, and how the man should ensure that the marriage still takes place. He might convince a female companion of the girl to bring her to his house unbeknownst to the girl, and he can then do the marriage ceremony as discussed above. Or, if the girl is about to be married to another man, he can disparage that man to her parents until her parents instruct her to marry him instead.

A man could also become friends with the girl's brother and assist him with his love life, which will gain the brother's favor and convince him that his sister should marry the man. The brother will then bring her to the man's house, where the marriage ceremony can take place.

Lastly, Vatsyayana suggests that a man could have a female companion of the girl get her drunk, have her brought to the man so that he can take advantage of her while she is asleep, and then she will need to marry him. This last option is hopefully not one that would be used by modern-day followers of the *Kama Sutra*.

Vatsyayana finishes the section with a verse that describes how each form of marriage listed is a better choice than the one that comes after it and that only when no other option is available, should a man follow the least desirable form of marriage. "In all the forms of marriage given in this chapter of work, the one that precedes is better than the one that follows it on account of its being more in accordance with the commands of religion, and therefore it is only when it is impossible to carry the former into practice that the latter should be resorted to. As the fruit of all good marriages is love, the Gandharva form or marriage is respected, even though it is formed under unfavorable circumstances, because it fulfills the object sought for. Another cause of the respect accorded to the Gandharva form of marriage is that it brings forth happiness, causes less trouble in its performance than the other forms of marriage, and is above all the result of previous love."

The third book focuses almost exclusively on marriage, and "even if we disregard certain magical aspects, there is much to be said for paying some attention to the qualities that the Kama Sutra suggests are desirable in a wife." The most compelling of these qualities is "confidence," or the idea that a man must dispel the fear of sex in the virgin bride before engaging in sexual union. It's a remarkable diversion from what has come to be known as the ancient tradition of the "wedding night," where a virgin bride is deflowered after enduring pain and fear in the fulfillment of her "duties" as a wife. Instead, says Vatsyayana, a man must take his time with his new wife before even thinking about initiating sexual intercourse. They must spend a considerable amount of time together, getting to know one another. Then they should discuss sex using soft words, move on to subtle advances, and finally, after ten days or more, initiate the first sexual union.

For all its gentle treatment of the matter of sexuality, the Kama Sutra does depart from this approach to make categorical lists of undesirable qualities - even to the point of stipulating the types of girls who cannot be married. Some of these qualities include: an ill-sounding name; upturned nostrils; glandular enlargements; disfigurements; and sweaty palms or feet. These lists are enough to make any female reader angry, but the Kama Sutra is not in and of itself a misogynistic text.

What is perhaps more worthy of examination is the subtle deceit that the author encourages in men. The Kama Sutra, despite its occasional diversions into biological classifications (penis size, emission-amount matching, etc.), also rewards those who pursue their loves to no end. The author offers a laundry list of suggestions that a man should follow if he wishes to marry the woman he loves, not many of which are particularly ethical (sabotaging the competition, creating false witnesses to offer praise in front of the bride's family, etc.). The words "acquired" and "acquisition" are used several times, suggesting that it is a man's duty to "acquire" the one he loves through hard work. Far from urging men to wait to find their "one true love," the Kama Sutra argues that nothing can be achieved without careful negotiation.

As a result, wooing is given quite a lot of attention in the text, and the male is given a precise set of instructions to this end. If in previous books we saw the somewhat alarming list of things that women must be good at in order to attract a mate, now we see what a man must be able to do - procure gifts, show off his talents, teach his mate the 64 means of achieving pleasure, etc. More than anything, he must be a subtle observer of behavior, carefully reading his chosen female to determine when and if she loves him, when and if she's ready for further courtship, when and if she's ready for sex, and when and if she's ready for marriage. It is this emphasis on reading behavior that makes the Kama Sutra so remarkable - it is not a sexual manual, but rather a love manual. And the first step to finding love and maintaining (and consummating) it is being fully aware of a lover's behavior, and accounting for all insecurities, hesitations, and fears.

There is one odd ambiguity in this book: the question of when, exactly, a man is permitted to have sex with a girl. In the beginning of the chapter, especially in light of all the instructions for building confidence in a woman, there is the implication that sex comes after marriage - specifically, more than ten days after marriage. But later on, during the discussion about men who must convince women that they can be suitable husbands, the author seems to suggest that a man should have sex with a woman as a way of coercing her to marry him. These apparent contradictions might be traced to either the idea that Vatsyayana is collecting anecdotes and wisdom from different sources or - perhaps more likely - that he is accounting for different ways of ensnaring a wife given different circumstances.

Charlotte Brown

Chapter 5
Part IV – About a Wife

In this part, Vatsyayana discusses the proper conduct of a woman once she is married. This includes housekeeping, behavior toward her husband and other people, purchasing household goods, and entertaining guests. Vatsyayana also tackles how an elder wife should conduct herself toward younger wives, and how the younger wives should conduct themselves toward the elder wife.

A virtuous woman who has affection for her husband should treat him as if he were a divine being, and thus take care of his whole family. In the house, the husband is a god. The wife should keep the house clean, arrange flowers for decoration, and keep the floors smooth and polished. She should also do all the religious poojas necessary, for nothing attracts the heart more than "careful observance of the household rituals." The wife should plant and tend an herb garden, and should carefully maintain family relations. She should avoid the company of female beggars, female fortunetellers, and witches. She should consider her husband's likes and dislikes when preparing his food, and whenever she hears his footsteps at home she should be ready to do his bidding, including washing his feet. Whenever she goes anywhere with her husband she should put on ornaments, and she should not accept invitations, attend marriages, sit with her friends, or visit temples without his permission. In the same way, she should always sit down after him, get up before him, and never awaken him when he is asleep. She should forgive him when he misbehaves and not use abusive language, for there is nothing worse to a husband than a scolding wife.

A wife, moreover, should not tell strangers the amount of her wealth, not the secrets that her husband confides to her. She should surpass all the women of her own rank in cleverness, appearance, and cooking skills. Additionally, she should make sure the expenditures of the household are in accordance with the family income, and should make sure that oil, sugar, and butter are all prepared at home.

Her duties also include looking after the tilling of the fields, keeping the flock, and taking care of domestic animals.

When her husband is on a journey, a virtuous woman should wear only her most auspicious ornaments, and should observe the fasts in honor of the gods. While anxious to hear news of her husband, she should still be mindful of the household affairs and ensure that the house is ready for his return. When he returns, she should receive him in her ordinary clothes so that he may know in what way she has lived during his absence, and should bring him presents as well as materials for the worship of the deity.

A woman only remarries when she is ill-tempered, disliked by her husband, desirous of offspring, continually giving birth to daughters, or suffering from her husband's impotence. From the beginning, a wife aims to win her husband's heart through his devotion, good temper, and wisdom, but if she bears no children, she should tell her husband to marry another woman. When the second wife is brought to the house, the first wife should give her a position superior to her own, and look upon her as a sister. If the younger wife does anything to displease the husband, the elder wife should always be ready to give her careful advice. The younger wife, meanwhile, should regard the elder wife as her "mother," and should not give away any secrets without her knowledge. Indeed, she should not even approach her husband without the permission of the elder wife. No matter how much she resents a rival wife, this younger wife cannot tell her husband of her pain.

An abandoned or neglected wife should never rebuke her husband or show obstinacy; she should only go near her husband when it is agreeable to him. She should keep her husband's weak points secret and show her children that she is devoted to their father. Meanwhile, should a woman become widowed, she cannot remarry unless she is of poor circumstances or a weak nature.

On the Manner of Living of a Virtuous Woman, and of Her Behavior During the Absence of her Husband

According to Vatsyayana, it is the duty of a wife to maintain the household. She must keep it clean and smelling fresh, tend the garden, and ensure that materials are prepared for the daily sacrifices. She should make him meals that he enjoys and that are good for him, and be prepared to obey the commands that he gives to her. A wife should always make sure that the house is stocked with necessary items, including foods, household goods, and materials for sacrifices. She may go out in public only with her husband's consent. A wife should make sure to avoid certain people, including female beggars, unchaste women, female fortune tellers, and witches.

If a man misbehaves, the wife may inform him of her displeasure, but should not use overly scolding or abusive language, particularly in front of his friends. She also should not sulk.

On a daily basis, a woman should ensure that she is clean and dressed appropriately, with simple clothing and limited ornamentation and scents. When a woman wishes to approach her husband for an intimate encounter, however, she should increase her use of ornamentation and perfume, and should wear a colorful dress.

Vatsyayana goes into a fair amount of detail of the items the wife should ensure are kept in the home, how meals are to be cooked, and how to keep the household. This includes ensuring that her in-laws are always welcome and taken care of when they visit and that she be generous with her servants, as long as her husband is aware of the generosity in advance.

When a man goes away on a journey, a wife should continue to maintain the household, and should not go out in public except on special occasions, such as a birth or death. When he returns, rather than greeting him dressed in special attire, a woman should be wearing her daily clothing and ornamentation so that her husband will know how she lived while he was gone.

It would seem from this section that while there is much emphasis on the power and importance that a woman plays in sexual encounters, and ensuring that a woman is pleased during those times in the daily life of a married couple, it is the man who holds the power and authority in the relationship.

Vatsyayana summarizes this section with a verse on the duties of the wife, and what complying with those duties will gain her: "The wife, whether she be a woman of a noble family, or a virgin widow remarried, or a concubine, should lead a chaste life, devoted to her husband, and doing everything for his welfare. Women acting thus acquire Dharma, Artha, and Kama, obtain a high position, and generally keep their husbands devoted to them."

On the Conduct of the Elder Wife Towards the Other Wives of her Husband, and on That of a Younger Wife Towards the Elder Ones. Also on the Conduct of a Virgin Widow Re-Married; of a Wife Disliked by her Husband; of the Women in the King's Harem; and Lastly on the Conduct of a Husband Toward Many Wives

During her life, there are a few reasons why a woman may end up being remarried. These reasons may be a problem for the husband, the wife, or both, and include ill-temper of the wife, the husband's dislike of the wife, an inability to produce children, producing only girl children, or impotence of the husband (inability to perform sexually).

If a woman is unable to give her husband children or is unable to produce a male child, then she should assist her husband in attracting a second wife. When a second wife comes into the home, the elder wife should look upon her as a sister, and should ensure that the younger wife conducts herself in a way that is pleasing to the husband. The elder wife should treat any children as her own.

If there are more than two wives, the elder wife should associate primarily with the wife who is immediately after her in rank and age. If there is a favorite, other than the wife closest to the elder wife, she should scheme with the other wives against the favorite, and should encourage her husband to choose a different favorite, although she should not do so openly and obviously.

A younger wife should view the elder wife as her mother and should not approach the husband without the elder wife's permission. She should never complain to the husband about any mistreatment that she receives from the elder wife, and should sympathize with the elder wife if the husband dislikes or disregards her.

In the *Kama Sutra*, the term "widow" does not mean a woman whose husband has died. Rather, it simply means a woman who is no longer married to her husband for any reason. A widow remarried is a widow who has remarried due to poor circumstances during her widowhood, and is also referred to as a virgin widow. In speaking about virgin widows, Vatsyayana notes that previous scholars, including Babhravya and Gonardiya, argue that widows should be careful about the men they remarry to ensure financial stability rather than happiness or love. Vatsyayana, on the other hand, believes that a widow should marry whichever man she loves and believes will make her happy.

When a woman remarries, her husband will likely pay for the costs of the party, but she may do so if she would like to and has the means. If the woman has voluntarily left her former marriage, she should return any gifts that were given to her by her first husband, aside from mutual presents which were exchanged by the husband and wife. However, if it was not her choice to leave the marriage, then she is entitled to keep all of her possessions.

Once remarried, a woman will live in the household as one of the chief members of the family, and should make sure to be kind to other members of the house, including other wives, servants, and friends and family. She should work to establish herself as an excellent wife, accomplished in the sixty-four arts of love, and be obedient to her husband's commands.

If a woman is disliked by her husband (whether a widow or not), she should try to make friends with the wife who is most liked, so as to learn from that wife how to please their husband. She should work to make herself as pleasing as possible, to hopefully regain his affections.

All of these conduct requirements apply equally to women in the king's harem. The king also has certain expectations of conduct that he is expected to follow. In the afternoon, the king should dress and ornament himself, then visit with his wives, carrying on a conversation with them and entertaining them to show respect and affection. After he visits the harem, he should visit any virgin widows that he may have, then the concubines and dancing girls. Each of these types of women should be visited in separate rooms.

After the king's midday nap, he will get up and choose which wife is to spend the night with him. A female servant will then go and advise the wife and prepare her. If a wife has had her turn missed, or could not go to the king for her turn due to having her period, then that wife's servant may approach the king with ointments on behalf of the wife to see if the king will change his mind. Once the king has made his decision, the chosen wife will be informed that her ointment was accepted and that it will be her turn to spend the night with the king.

When a man, whether a king or not, has many wives, he should treat them equally as much as he is able. He should not talk negatively about one wife to another, and he should reprimand any wife who speaks badly about another wife.

Of all the books of the Kama Sutra, this is perhaps the one that seems the most anti-feminist. A woman is placed squarely at the head of domestic matters and in a role of servitude to her husband. That said, Hinduism has never shied away from the fact that it sees a woman's control of her house as an immense source of power and responsibility. It is up to the woman to keep the husband afloat and to ensure that he fulfills his worth as a man by keeping the family together, charming his relatives, making sure that the family is fed, managing the expenses, and having children. For all the anti-feminist overtones, the subtext is that the woman is responsible for the family's livelihood.

At the same time, it is quite clear that a wife's chief responsibility is to bear children - and, specifically, to bear sons. If a woman cannot bear children, then the husband - in a radical departure from everything else in the Kama Sutra - is allowed to remarry. Not only is he allowed to remarry; the first wife must take care of the younger wife in order to ensure that their husband produces children. This is technically polygamy, of course, but the Kama Sutra presents the arrangement as a solely functional endeavor - a way of making up for the first wife's failings.

Ideally, there is a great deal of trust between man and wife. There are repeated mentions of the fact that women should not betray their husbands by sharing their secrets - either to family members, people outside the family, or to a second wife if one is brought into the house. Moreover, the husband needs to know that his wife is like the rock of the house - faithful, loyal, and always attentive to her duties. Thus, the Kama Sutra preaches even the smallest details of fidelity, such as wearing casual home clothes upon a husband's return from a long journey in order to show him that the home has been cared for in his absence.

There is certainly room for disagreements between a husband and a wife, but if a wife is ill-tempered or if her husband truly cannot stand her, then the Kama Sutra allows for separation or remarriage. However, if the disagreement is one-sided (for example, if the husband can't stand his wife, but the wife is still in love with her husband), then the implication is that the wife should simply stay as far away from the husband as she can while performing her wifely duties.

The question of widowhood has long been a subject of debate in Hinduism, especially as modern pragmatism encroaches on ancient tradition. But the Kama Sutra suggests that there are only two good reasons for a widow to remarry. One is if she is of "poor circumstances" and needs a man to ensure that her livelihood remains intact. In other words, the man suddenly becomes the source of a woman's survival - which is in direct contrast to the earlier part of the chapter, which suggests that a man is dependent on his wife for his sustenance. The second condition under which remarriage is possible is if a widow is of "weak character," but what constitutes a weak character is never explained. We are left with the understanding that if a woman knows that this pejorative term "weak" comes with her desire to remarry after being left a widow, she will refrain from doing so.

Charlotte Brown

Chapter 6
Part V – About the Wives of Other People

Unlike most modern societies, it would appear from the *Kama Sutra,* that ancient Hindu culture did not frown on becoming romantically or sexually involved with another man's wife. Part I of the *Kama Sutra* briefly discusses being sexually involved with another man's wife, but this part is focused on becoming involved in a romantic way.

According to Vatsyayana, a man may become involved with another man's wife when he realizes that his love for her has increased in intensity. In the *Kama Sutra*, the intensity of love is measured in ten different degrees. The signs of these degrees, in order of increasing intensity, are:

- Love of the eye – enjoying how a woman looks;

- Attachment of the mind – thinking about the woman as more than a fleeting fancy;
- Constant reflection – being unable to stop thinking about the woman;
- Destruction of sleep;
- Emaciation of the body;
- Turning away from objects of enjoyment – not being able to take pleasure in anything;
- Removal of shame – being willing to do anything to gain the woman's affection;
- Madness;
- Fainting;
- Death.

Previous works that had been studied by Vatsyayana stated that a woman's personality and character traits could be determined from the appearance of her body. Vatsyayana, on the other hand, felt that physical characteristics were fleeting and easily changed and that women should be judged by their conduct.

When a married woman is approached by another man who is interested in her sexually or romantically, there are a number of reasons why she may choose to refuse his advances. These reasons include love for her husband, difference in rank, distrust of his genuineness, and fear of discovery, as well as many others listed by Vatsyayana. If a man can determine why a woman has rejected him, he may be able to overcome that difficulty. Vatsyayana sets out a long list of the kind of men who are most likely to succeed in wooing the wife of another man, and the type of woman who is most likely to enter into an extramarital affair.

Vatsyayana ends this section with a verse about the desire and the ability of men to win over women: "Desire, which springs from nature, and which is increased by art, and from which all danger is taken away by wisdom, becomes firm and secure. A clever man, depending on his own ability, and observing carefully the ideas and thoughts of women, and removing the causes of their turning away from men, is generally successful with them."

Before a man consorts with another man's wife, he should consider a number of things - the possibility of actually making the woman his wife, her fitness for sexual congress, the danger that the union might pose to himself, and the future effects of this union. Indeed, a man may see that he needs the wife of another in order to preserve his own life, since his love for her far exceeds his love for his current wife. If a man finds himself besieged by attachment of the mind, constant reflection, emaciation, loss of will, turning away from pleasure and enjoyment, shameless behavior, mental imbalance, fainting fits, or even no will to live, then he should pursue the wife of another.

Ancient sages argued that a man could tell the character of a woman from her body and movements, but Vatsayayana believes that making these judgments will likely lead to terrible errors, and that women should be judged mainly by their conduct, the outward expressions of their thoughts, and the movements of their bodies. Men and women, moreover, differ in their psychological approaches to love. A woman loves "without regard to right or wrong" and will naturally shrink from a man, until she is repeatedly courted - at which point she will consent. A man, however, will become indifferent whether his advances are rejected or not as his feelings are easily dispatched.

A woman will reject a man if she already has a husband, is angry about their differences with regards to social status, doesn't like his cleverness, thinks the man is too devoted to his friends, or is fearful of his strength or political position.

If a man senses that any of these are possible reasons for a woman's disdain, he should seek to comfort her and let her know that these perceptions are in error. For instance, if a woman thinks that a man is of low character, he should remove this perception by showing his valor and his wisdom. If she is afraid of him, then he should give her proper encouragement and comfort.

At a first meeting, a man should be careful to look at a woman in a way that makes his mind known to her, but at the same time he should listen to her with indifference in order to inspire her desire. He can even go so far as to subtly show off to her by engaging a third person in conversation about subjects he knows she will want to hear about. Indeed, it wouldn't be out of place to embrace and kiss a young boy in order to send covert signals to the woman. Once he has engaged a woman, there is a complex set of steps he should take to slowly make her acquaintance. He should gradually increase his visits to her, first engaging her on a business level and then on a more personal one, before initiating physical intimacy or voicing his desire for marriage. A man should only seduce one woman at a time.

There are several ways for a man to determine the "fitness" of a woman's mind. If she meets him once, and then comes to their second meeting better dressed than she was before, he can be certain that she is capable of "being enjoyed by the use of a little force." If a woman avoids the attentions of a man, and on account of respect for him or herself will not meet or approach him, a man can get her to surrender either by persistence or by using a friend as a mediator. If a woman reproaches a man for his advances, she should be ignored completely (unless these reproaches are done flirtatiously).

Vatsyayana now turns his attentions to the behavior of the nobles. A king, for instance, is constantly watched and imitated, so his behavior must be beyond reproach. A king, after all, has numerous wives, so when he desires a woman, it is best if his wife introduces her to him - perhaps by inviting her to the royal palace so that she might see the practice of the art that she has been invited to perform with the king. A king also has powers of force, so if the woman desired by the king is living with a person who is not her husband, the king can have her arrested and made a slave.

The women of the royal house cannot see or meet with men because they are guarded and must deal with the dissatisfaction that inevitably arises when one's husband is shared with many wives. As a result, the women of the royal house must learn to give pleasure to each other. In dire circumstances, they can have young men delivered to the palace dressed as girls for them to enjoy.

About Making Acquaintance with the Woman, and of the Efforts to Gain her Over

Some of the authors on whose works Vatsyayana based the *Kama Sutra* believed that, while unmarried women were best courted by men directly, it was better to approach married women through a female messenger. Vatsyayana, however, felt that it was also best for a man to approach a woman directly if possible, regardless of whether or not she was married. Vatsyayana completely dismissed the idea that certain women, who were bolder and spoke more freely, would be more easily wooed by men directly than those women who were shyer and quieter.

To court a married woman, a man would need to encounter her in one of two ways according to Vatsyayana: either a natural opportunity or a special opportunity. A natural opportunity was when the man would go to the woman's house, or the other way around, whereas a special opportunity was one where they would meet at a friend's house or at a celebration of a special event.

Once in the woman's company, a man should be clear of his intentions toward her, by using body language to indicate his attraction. He should look at her, talk pleasantly about her to mutual friends, and present himself in a way that will hopefully attract her. A particularly useful strategy, if there is a child present, is to conduct a conversation with the woman through the child, avoiding direct contact with the woman while still interacting with her. As the connection grows, the man's wife should become involved, getting to know the woman and becoming friends with her. He should give the woman gifts as appropriate, and request tokens of affection in return. If the woman returns his interest, he will reach a point where it is appropriate to touch and embrace the woman, and eventually will engage in sexual acts with her.

Vatsyayana notes that while a man is trying to seduce one woman, he should not be pursuing any other. However, once he has secured the first woman's affection and spent some time with her as a lover, he can then start to court another woman if he finds one that he would like to pursue.

To protect his reputation, a man should try to avoid seducing a woman who is nervous, untrustworthy, or who has a mother-in-law or father-in-law who could discover and disapprove of the arrangement.

Examination of the State of a Woman's Mind

When attempting to seduce a married woman, a man should be very careful to study and be aware of the woman's state of mind. If she is willing to listen to his advances but does not provide a reply, then she is open to the possibility, but may be more comfortable making arrangements through a female messenger. If she meets him again and is dressed in a more pleasing way than she was previously, this is a sign that she is interested in entering into a relationship with the man. If a woman avoids the man's attentions and will not meet with him, then she will likely be difficult or impossible to win over, and the man should look elsewhere. If a woman responds to a man's advances with harsh words, then he should abandon his efforts immediately.

According to Vatsyayana, there are certain actions that a woman can take that will make it clear that she welcomes a man's advances and is interested in pursuing the matter further. These actions include calling out to the man without him addressing her first, speaking to him with a trembling voice, sweating, and touching his body in an innocent but prolonged manner.

Overall, a man should first arrange to be introduced to a woman, and then carry on a conversation with her. From there he can start the courtship process discussed above, and will either stop the process if at some point he receives a sign that the woman is not interested, or will pursue the courtship to the point of a relationship being established if the woman is interested in him.

About the Business of a Go-Between

When a married woman shows interest in being courted, but then the man does not see her again, he may choose a messenger, or go-between, to assist him in his courtship of her. The go-between, who will be a female friend of the man, must work to gain the confidence of the woman and become her friend as well. Once this is accomplished, she should talk to the woman about her husband, and discuss her husband's negative qualities and the suitor's positive ones. If it is a woman's first extramarital affair, this will likely be more successful if the go-between is someone who she already knows and is trusted to some degree, as she will likely be more difficult to persuade into having an affair.

Eventually, the go-between should tell the woman about the man's affection, and explain how madly in love he is with her. The go-between will be able to assess whether the woman is interested, and will be able to communicate that to the man. If the woman is interested in the man, she will be willing to have these discussions with the go-between, and will make attempts to meet up with the go-between in places where her husband will not be present so that they can discuss the suitor.

Once the woman's interest has been confirmed, the go-between can then play the role of transporting tokens of affection between the man and woman. Once presents have been exchanged, the go-between will assist the man and woman in arranging for them to meet up with each other. According to Babhravya, an earlier Hindu scholar, this first meeting after determination of affection should take place during a special occasion such as a wedding, funeral, fair, or party, or when going to the river to bathe. Gonikaputra, on the other hand, felt that the meeting should occur in the home of a mutual female friend, or an astrologer or holy person. Vatsyayana, however, believed that all that was required was that the meeting place could be easily accessed and that arrangements had been made to avoid discovery.

According to Vatsyayana, there are several different types of go-betweens, depending on how involved the person is in the man and woman's affairs. The most in-depth involvement is that of a go-between who, after seeing that a man and woman feel some initial attraction for or interest in each other, brings them together on her own initiative, and is fully involved in the entire business. Then there is a go-between who is involved in only a limited part of the affair, for example, if some of the advances have already been made by the man. The bearer of a letter is a go-between who merely transports communications between the man and woman.

In rare cases, a woman may act as a go-between for herself. In this situation, she will approach the man and indicate her interest. A woman is also considered to be acting as a go-between for herself if she agrees to approach a man for some other woman, and then approaches him on her own behalf instead. A man can be a similar type of go-between if he agrees to act as another man, then approaches the woman on his own behalf.

In some circumstances, an innocent young wife is friends with another woman, and that woman gains information from the young wife about what the husband likes and desires and then teaches the young wife how to give that to her husband. In this case, the innocent young wife is considered to be acting as a go-between for herself, although she was unaware that she was doing so.

A man may use his own wife as a go-between to approach another woman, although he should be careful to choose a wife that he can trust to represent him positively and not discourage the other woman from being interested in her husband.

Finally, when a man sends a female servant to the woman under some false pretense and hides a secret message or token in the item being sent, then the servant is acting as a mute go-between.

The types of women who are appropriate to use as go-betweens include female astrologers, female beggars, female servants, or female artists, as well as already existing friends, servants, or wives.

About the Love of Persons in Authority for the Wives of Other Men

In this section, Vatsyayana discusses how a king is to deal with a situation where he is interested in the wife of another man. Just as with any man, there may be times when a king may find himself in this situation, but for a king, it is more difficult because he is always under observation and cannot simply visit a woman's home without there being a great deal of public attention.

During certain festival times of the year, women of the cities and towns (usually friends or family of the harem women) would be permitted to visit the women in the king's harem. They would spend the night in the harem's quarters, and return to their homes in the morning. If the king were interested in one of these women, he could instruct a female attendant to approach that woman as she was leaving the harem's quarters, and invite her to tour the palace. Once the female attendant was able to get the woman alone, she could advise her of the king's interest. The woman would be completely entitled to refuse the king's advances, in which case the female attendant would provide her with sumptuous gifts and send her on her way with well-wishes. If the woman was interested, the female attendant would then take her for a meeting with the king.

If a king desired a woman who was not interested, or whose husband would not permit her to visit the palace, then the king would have the option of creating a quarrel with the husband. The king could then have the woman arrested for being the wife of an enemy, and she could be placed into the king's harem. This would, of course, be a less desirable option than having the woman willingly come to the king.

Regardless of how a king arranges for another man's wife to be his lover, there is one technique that he should never use. According to Vatsyayana, a king should never enter another person's home as there is too much risk to the king, which would then mean danger for the king's people if something were to happen to the king. This concern is summarized by a verse at the end of this part: "The above and other ways are the means employed in different countries by kings with regard to the wives of other persons. But a king, who has the welfare of his people at heart, should not on any account put them into practice."

About the Women of the Royal Harem; and of the Keeping of One's Own Wife

Women in the king's harem were not permitted to have male visitors, or to see men other than the king. Also, the women would be part of a harem, share their husband with many other wives and with courtesans as well. As a result, it was apparently a common problem for the women of the harem to be sexually frustrated with limited or no ability to be satisfied by their husband. The women, therefore, would come up with ways to still participate in sexual acts and achieve sexual release.

One way in which the women of the harem would get sexually satisfied would be to dress their friends or attendants like men, and the "men" would then use fruits or vegetables in the shape of a lingam to satisfy the women. The women of the harem might also use the statue of a male figure which happened to have an erect lingam.

Some kings might take medications that would allow them to have sex with multiple wives a night, although not all kings were willing or able to do so even with medication.

Particularly brave women of the harem would disguise a male lover as a woman and then have him brought into the harem's quarters. The women's female attendants would assist with this by providing the men with the information about how to access the living quarters and the guard and attendant schedule of the women. In this case, it would be common for several of the women to take the man as a lover, because there would be less risk of one man being caught than of several men coming into the quarters to see different women.

In the first discussion of magic in the *Kama Sutra*, Vatsyayana describes a mixture which, if made and applied to the body, was supposed to make the man invisible, including to the harem's guards. This mixture involved the heart of an ichneumon (mongoose), the eyes of a serpent, and the fruit of a long gourd. All of the ingredients were to be burnt without letting the smoke get away. The ashes were then to be ground and mixed in equal parts with water. Then the man would then apply the mixture to his eyes, and would allegedly be invisible to the guards.

The best way for a man to access the harem's quarters would include times when goods were being delivered and brought into the palace, when festivals were taking place, or when the king was away on a pilgrimage. At all of these times, there would be less attention on the women's quarters, either because there was so much activity going on or because the king was away and most of his attendants would be with him.

Due to the likelihood of women of the harem taking male lovers when their king fails to keep them satisfied, Vatsyayana offered certain recommendations for how a king should conduct himself to avoid this situation. He mentions that previous authors had stated that the sentinels chosen by the king to guard his harem should have been tested and proved to be free of carnal desire so that they are not tempted to become involved with the women themselves. They should also have been tested to ensure that they can resist the temptation to accept money or other tokens, or to give into fear upon being threatened if another person is attempting to access the harem.

Vatsyayana completed this section with a verse cautioning men about how to guard their wives: "A clever man, learning from the Shastras the ways of winning over the wives of other people, is never deceived in the case of his own wives. No one, however, should make use of these ways for seducing the wives of others, because they do not always succeed, and moreover, often cause disasters, and the destruction of the Dharma and Artha. This book, which is intended for the good of the people, and to teach them the ways of guarding their own wives, should not be made use of merely for gaining over the wives of others."

This book again emphasizes a woman's behavior, not her external appearance, which is one of the hallmarks of the Kama Sutra. Vatsyayana lays out a series of prescriptions for a man's approach of a woman, and delineates what he should do in each case of behavior. In general, the author sees woman as eminently conquerable, believing that they are biologically wired to submit after multiple advances. This does make sense to some degree, as the book subtly implies that women must be quite sure of their mate before they relent. Only a man who repeatedly shows dedication and commitment to a woman will inspire her to relinquish her power.

At the same time, however, men tend to be indifferent after rejection, and thus the Kama Sutra is a necessary guide to ensure that men stay persistent after women spurn them. Vatsyayana writes that it is a man's nature to give up and a woman's nature to resist, and without this understanding of each other there will be no ultimate victory, only a settling of scores that leaves dissatisfied parties. The only reason to give up on a woman after her initial rejection is if she reproaches a man without any sign of love; then it is not a match.

Some of the ways Vatsyayana suggests a man should win over a woman may sound ridiculous to modern ears (for example, kissing young boys in front of her in order to arouse her!), but he is simply referring to man's age-old tendency to show off for the women they desire. Indeed, what is so remarkable about the Kama Sutra is that it does not see love as a holy act of union that requires patience and endurance but rather as an art of manipulation, pride, and even deceit. Like birds that puff up their chests in preparation for the mating game, Vatsyayana encourages men to pursue their women like warriors - with their full attention on the battle ahead.

Submission is a word that appears repeatedly throughout the Kama Sutra, and it is one that seems to have biological resonance. The more advanced a species is, the more complex its mating rituals. Many mammals are notably finicky about their mates, but the characteristic of a female submitting after many advances is quite consistent - and it would make sense that a female, when pressed repeatedly, will submit to a man who pursues her and persuades her that they are meant to be together. The concept of the Casanova seems to emanate from this line of thinking - the lover who is so good with words and the dance of courtship that no woman can resist his charms.

While ordinary mortals must rely on courtship, the king has to deal with his own set of codes. As he is a model for all of his subjects, he cannot do anything prurient, and is thus encouraged to rely on go-betweens and his wives to acquire new women. Little is said about the practice of polygamy, but we must assume that kings are permitted (even encouraged) to take multiple wives in order to ensure the maximum number of male progeny. The king certainly can use his power to squire a girl, and Vatsyayana suggests that if he can't acquire a girl because she is already married, that he should simply use force to imprison her and bring her into the worldly court. This may seem malicious, but the suggestion is merely an extension of the larger theme of this book: a male must pursue the object of his desire relentlessly until she finally submits, ultimately loving him the more for his unflagging determination.

Chapter 7

Part VI – About Courtesans

In the translation of the *Kama Sutra* by Sir Richard Francis Burton (discussed in greater detail later in the book), Sir Burton included an introduction to this part which stated that this was one of the most in-depth and thorough examinations of the ways of courtesans, despite it having been written almost 2000 years earlier. He also noted that the courtesan was an important part of Hindu society, and applauded the Hindus for recognizing courtesans as such. In fact, he went so far as to disparage the Western cultures for treating courtesans with such brutality and contempt compared to the Eastern cultures, such as the Hindus.

The sixth book of the Kama Sutra discusses the courtesan, delineating her role, her responsibilities, and even the workings of her mind. According to Vatsyayana, the courtesan (or vaishika) has long been a key element of human society, and particularly Hindu culture. Indeed, as long as they behave with decency and propriety, they can often earn considerable respect, unlike in the West, where they are treated with brutality and contempt. Courtesans in the Hindu culture are not considered "prostitutes" as such, and in the past have been educated and trained to become amusing escorts for high-class men. Indeed, says the Kama Sutra, seeming to wink to its audience, every woman "has got an inkling of the profession in her nature," for as a general rule a woman aims "to make herself agreeable to the male sex."

Intercourse with men offers courtesans not only a livelihood, but also sexual pleasure. If a courtesan takes up with a man for love, she can slip back into the role of a lover, but when she takes up with a man only for money, her lovemaking is artificial, even forced by her. However, it is a courtesan's duty to act as if she is in love during every encounter, as her partner's confidence relies on the idea that she is in love with him, regardless of the circumstances under which they have come together.

A courtesan should sit or stand at the door to her house and look out on the outside world, like an object on display for sale. At the same time, she should make friends with people who will protect her, such as guards of the town, police officers, court members, astrologers, and powerful men. A courtesan should try to take up with young, handsome men who are free from any ties and already have their livelihoods. They can even take up with a man who has feminine traits and wants to be thought of as a man. A courtesan should be beautiful, enjoy sex, have a firm mind, be interested in meeting new people and acquiring experience and knowledge, and be free from avarice. A courtesan should avoid men who are sickly, affected by parasites, have bad breath, are greedy, are thieves, or are conceited. A courtesan should not sacrifice money for love, because money is her top priority. If she does fall in love, however, she should be careful not to immediately consent to a union, for men are "apt to despise things which are easily acquired."

When a courtesan is with a lover, she should behave like a chaste woman and do everything for his satisfaction. At the same time, she should give him pleasure without becoming attached to him. She can do this in a number of ways, and can even invent a harsh or nagging mother who can forcibly take her away from her lover whenever he's drawing too close. The courtesan can "show pretended anger, dejection, fear and shame" at having to leave him on the account of such a nag, but in private she should continue these schemes in order to ensure her independence. When she is with a man, a courtesan should show him the 64 kinds of pleasure, conceal her personal feelings and reveal only her love for him, follow his lead in terms of mood, express curiosity about his wives, give him confidence by revealing how attractive he is to women, and attending on him with praise and wit.

A courtesan makes money either through natural and lawful means, or through artifice. Sages reveal that a courtesan should not use artifice unless she absolutely has to, or can get double or triple the money from her lover. Artifice can include taking money from her lover ostensibly to buy clothes, flowers, or food, and then using less than the amount given, or praising his intelligence so that he must give her gifts connected with the vows of the holidays. She can also claim that her body or home has been robbed, contract debts that her lover must pay, or demand the assistance of her friends and family.

A courtesan can easily see when a man's desire is cooling, as he will give her less money than she wants, make false promises, forget her promises, or sleep with someone else under the pretense of doing something for a friend. When a courtesan finds that her lover's disposition is changing, she should get possession of all his best things before he becomes aware of her intentions and then get rid of him by belittling his pride. A courtesan should only return to a former lover if he has acquired new wealth and is still attached to her enough to want her back.

A courtesan should not confine herself to a single lover, lest she risk losing valuable money. However, if she can obtain tremendous financial gain from a single lover, she may consort with him alone. She should also, according to Vatsyayana, value gold over all other objects, since gold cannot be taken back, and can be exchanged for gifts. A courtesan may often find that she has to choose between two lovers - one who is generous and rich and one who is attached to her. Sages differ on which one she should choose but Vatsyayana argues that she should take the one who is more attached to her for he can be made to be generous. If a courtesan receives money from a man who is not her current lover, she risks falling out of her lover's good graces, forced union to a lower person, and even universal hatred.

Of the Causes of a Courtesan Resorting to Men; Of the Means of Attaching to Herself the Man Desired; And of the Kind of Man that it is Desirable to be Acquainted With

When Vatsyayana talks about courtesans "resorting to" men in this part, he is not talking about sexual relationships because courtesans would frequently be involved with men in a sexual way. Vatsyayana is referring to situations where a courtesan may choose to enter into a romantic relationship, whether for love or financial stability.

Vatsyayana advised that courtesans should make friendships with certain men, due to their ability to provide the courtesans with wealth and protect them from dangers. These men may not necessarily be ones with whom the women would be interested in having a romantic relationship but there would be some relationship formed that would help the courtesan. These types of men included police, officers of the court, learned men, and jesters. If a courtesan was interested in forming a relationship that would garner her wealth or at least financial stability, she should pursue men in the king's court, men of independent income, or the only son of a wealthy man, to name a few.

If a courtesan was truly interested in pursuing a romantic relationship with a man who could protect her and offer her wealth and love, she should look to men with particular characteristics, including: of high birth; learned and eloquent, affectionate with their family; sociable; strong and healthy; skilled in the sixty-four arts of love; and having an independent means of wealth or livelihood.

To increase the chances of success of attracting such a man, a courtesan should be beautiful and personable, enjoy sex and be a match for the man regarding sexual matters, should be eager to learn and experience new things, and should enjoy attending social gatherings.

These qualities were in addition to the qualities that all decent women were expected to have, which included intelligence, good disposition, speaking in a ladylike manner, and to know of the *Kama Sutra* and its associated arts.

Men who should always be avoided by courtesans for any relationship were those who were ill, unkind, greedy, untrustworthy, or too shy.

Previous writings on courtesans had stated that there were many circumstances which would cause a courtesan to decide that she wished to enter into a relationship with a man. Vatsyayana, however, felt that there were only three true causes: the desire for wealth; love; and to be free from misfortune.

Once a courtesan had selected the man that she wished to pursue, she could invite him to her house under the pretense of seeing some show, such as a cock fight. She would present the man with a gift when he arrived at the house and tell him stories to amuse him. Vatsyayana includes a verse which describes in greater detail how the courtesan should greet her potential lover: "When a lover comes to her abode, a courtesan should give him a mixture of betel leaves and betel nut, garlands of flowers, and perfumed ointments, and, showing her skill in arts, should entertain him with a long conversation. She should also give him some loving presents, and make an exchange of her own things with his, and at the same time should show him her skill in sexual enjoyment. When a courtesan is thus united with her lover, she should always delight him by affectionate gifts, by conversation, and by the application of tender means of enjoyment."

The courtesan's approach to pursuing a man is very different than that for an unmarried or married woman who is not a courtesan, as discussed in previous chapters because a courtesan would have been permitted to be much more forward in showing her interest and intentions.

Of Living Like a Wife

According to Vatsyayana, once a courtesan had chosen a lover, she should behave as though she was his wife, although she would not have the same right of attachment as an actual wife would. Vatsyayana sets out a long list of duties of the courtesan when acting like a wife, some of which are complimenting the man and enjoying sexual acts with him, sharing secrets and desires, supporting him in his wants and needs, never becoming too angry with him, and attending to him when he is sick. While the list is far too long to discuss in detail here, the overall premise is that the courtesan is there to satisfy and entertain the man when he wishes her to be, and to support him in all things.

Of the Means of Getting Money, of the Signs of the Change of a Lover's Feelings, and of the Way to Get Rid of Him

In this chapter, Vatsyayana discusses the ways in which a courtesan can obtain money from her lover. He notes that scholars before him had argued that a courtesan should not use artifice to get money if her lover is willing to provide her with whatever money she needs. Vatsyayana, however, believed that if a courtesan can get more money by using artifice, then she should do so.

Vatsyayana listed several ways in which a courtesan could trick her lover into giving her money, including asking for money to buy something, and then not purchasing it or purchasing it for less than was given to her; pretending to have had jewels stolen or lost, or property damaged, so that the lover will provide her with money to replace the items; pretending to be sick and having her lover provide her money for medicine and treatment, and telling her lover that his rivals had been more generous than him.

A courtesan could figure out when a lover was beginning to lose interest by the fact that he would become less willing to give money to her or pay for things. He might also be less passionate during sexual encounters, or promise to visit and then not show up. If a courtesan starts to believe that her lover is losing interest, she should make sure to get as much money from him as possible before he ends the relationship. If the man has little money to give her anyway, then she should end the relationship herself.

The *Kama Sutra* includes a list of many ways in which a courtesan could go about getting rid of her lover, including insulting him, refusing access to her body, being inactive during sex, interrupting him when he was talking, or laughing at him. All of these would be designed to make it clear to the lover that the courtesan was no longer interested in him. If none of these worked, the courtesan had the option of dismissing him outright.

Vatsyayana summarized this section with a verse on the duties of the courtesan: "The duty of a courtesan consists in forming connections with suitable men after due and full consideration, and attaching the person with whom she is united to herself; in obtaining wealth from the person who is attached to her, and then dismissing him after she has taken away all his possessions." According to Vatsyayana, courtesans were not only likely to act this way, but they were in fact expected to do so.

About Re-Union with a Former Lover

Once a courtesan had dismissed one lover or had the relationship ended by the lover, she would then be free to reunite with a former lover. This reunion would only be a recommended option if she had gained new wealth or still had a wealth of her own, and if the former lover was still interested in her. If the former lover was now living with another woman, Vatsyayana recommended that the courtesan think twice before attempting a reunion.

Whether a former lover was a good choice for reunion depended on several factors as discussed by Vatsyayana, mostly related to why he had left his former lover (and any lovers after that), or if they had left him, and whether he had wealth to offer her. If he had been the one to leave all of this former lovers, Vatsyayana suggested that he should be avoided because he was clearly too fickle. On the other hand, if all of his former lovers had left him, Vatsyayana cautioned that there was probably a reason why women kept leaving him, and perhaps he should be avoided.

When a courtesan had chosen a former lover for a reunion, then her female servant would be sent to provide some excuse as to why he had previously been dismissed by the courtesan. The female servant should speak kindly about the courtesan, and remind him of the happy times that he and the courtesan had enjoyed together.

If a courtesan found herself in a situation where she was choosing between two lovers, with one a former lover and one entirely new, Vatsyayana recommended that in most situations it would be better to choose the former lover because he was known to the courtesan. Essentially, this was an ancient form of the expression "better the devil you know, than the devil you don't."

In summary, Vatsyayana included the following verse: "'A wise woman should only renew her connection with a former lover if she is satisfied that good fortune, gain, love, and friendship, are likely to be the result of such a reunion.'"

Of Different Kinds of Gain

In this section, Vatsyayana discusses the different ways in which courtesans could make money, and which of those methods were preferable over others.

In the opinion of Vatsyayana, if a courtesan were able to make a good deal of money on a daily basis by entertaining multiple customers, then it would not make sense for her to commit herself to only one lover. On the other hand, if a lover were willing to provide an income equal to or greater than what she would make from multiple customers, then it would make sense to have just that one customer if the courtesan so desired.

Vatsyayana also recommended that, whenever a courtesan was given a chance between payment in gold and payment in other items, she should choose the gold. This was because gold could not be seen as a gift and taken back, and it could easily be used to procure other items wanted by the courtesan.

Vatsyayana did a thorough analysis of the different types of lovers whom a courtesan might encounter, and how she should choose among them. He believed that a lover who was emotionally attached should be chosen over one who was generous because an attached lover could be more easily persuaded to provide things due to his feelings for the courtesan. However, if choosing between a lover who was generous and one who was willing to do anything for the courtesan, Vatsyayana recommended choosing the generous lover in this case, because the one willing to do anything might consider his duty complete once he had done one thing that was requested of the courtesan, whereas the generous lover would be more likely to give to her on an ongoing basis. A grateful lover should be chosen over a liberal one because a liberal lover would be more likely to leave her.

Vatsyayana also had guidelines as to how a courtesan should spend her money, assuming that she made quite a bit of it. These suggestions included building temples or gardens, giving cows to Brahmans, and holding festivals in the honor of the gods. For less wealthy courtesans, he advised that they should spend their money on proper dress, food and drink, and pretty ornaments to adorn their body.

There may be reasons that a courtesan would be willing to provide her services for a lower rate for a certain man. This might be because she thinks he will improve her position, or he might assist her with some trouble that she is having, or she might truly be in love with him. For these reasons, it is acceptable that a courtesan would take less money from only that lover.

Vatsyayana's overall principle for courtesans was that they were to make as much money as they could in whichever way they could and that they should always choose to make money over other interests. This position makes sense, given that the courtesan's purpose within society was to make money from sex and not to have emotional attachments.

Of Gains and Losses; Attendant Gains and Losses; and Doubts; and Also of the Different Kinds of Courtesans

According to Vatsyayana, a loss could be the result of many different causes, such as too much pride, too much confidence, recklessness, or an accident. A courtesan should be careful to avoid these potential causes of loss.

Vatsyayana set out three types of gain or loss: wealth; religious merit; and pleasure. If one kind of gain was sought and another happened to come along with it, then that second gain was what Vatsyayana referred to as an attendant gain. When a courtesan was not sure whether she would receive a gain or not, this would be a simple doubt. When she was unsure as to which of two possibilities might happen, that would be a mixed doubt. Vatsyayana went through various examples of these different gains and losses so that a courtesan might see which situations could be beneficial to her and which would not be.

As to the different kinds of courtesans, according to Vatsyayana they were:

- A bawd;
- A female attendant;
- An unchaste woman;
- A dancing girl;
- A female artisan;
- A woman who has left her family;
- A woman living on her beauty; and
- A regular courtesan.

Each of these different kinds of courtesans would attract different types of men, and should use their own unique ways of attracting men and making money.

An entire book dedicated to the courtesan is certainly a surprise, given the fact that up until this point the Kama Sutra has focused on how an understanding between the sexes fosters love. A discussion about prostitution not only seems bizarre, but also antithetical. Right away, however, the author addresses this apparent contradiction, arguing that courtesans are crucial to the functioning of society, for they help men to gain confidence. It is a man's responsibility to give his partner confidence in the days after marriage, but how do men develop this confidence themselves?

This is the task of the courtesan: to develop her partner's confidence. She not only has the powers of the 64 sexual positions at her disposal, but she also possesses a keen insight into a man's psychology. A courtesan's primary objective is the acquisition of money, while a man's primary objectives are satiation of lust and love. In the gap between these two objectives there is room for negotiation, and the author lays out a series of strategies to help the courtesan determine exactly how to handle a male. Notice that the audience for this chapter is not the male, but rather the courtesan herself. As she is responsible for driving the action in this situation, it is natural that men are left out, just as women are essentially ignored in earlier portions of the work.

In many ways, the courtesan is responsible for a reversal of gender roles. For example, when the subjects of long-term attachment or a man's wives come up, it is her duty to act as the male typically would - nonchalant, impossible to pin down, uninterested in commitment. Even if she loves one of her partners, she would be wise to invent circumstances that would prevent her from being with him too frequently. She is, in many ways, a pillager, solely concerned with financial gain. If the courtesan falls in love, however, she must deal with the fact that the object of her affection is likely to harbor a deep mistrust towards her, and she must thus earn his confidence rather than vice versa.

Vatsyayana raises the question of what, exactly, a courtesan wants from an ideal lover: generosity? Extreme wealth? Obsession? He argues that a different goal characterizes each interaction. Generosity is the most useful, because a man who is generous to a courtesan will shower her with wealth without counting pennies or expecting favors in return. Extreme wealth is also useful, but if a man's attachment to a courtesan overwhelms his wealth, then he is likely to expect the courtesan to pay back every gift with some sort of sign of affection, which reduces the courtesan's power and ultimately ties her to one man.

Artifice - the idea that a woman must deceive her man in order to keep him happy - returns as a central concept here.

We saw elements of this earlier in the section that dealt with how a wife must approach her interactions with her husband, but this book suggests that a courtesan must employ all manner of deceit in order ensure that her lover continues to shower her with gifts and money. Because it is wealth, and not love, that is at stake, a courtesan must be extremely conscious of whether or not her lover's feelings are cooling off, and then quickly end the relationship before he can. These lists of signs that signal the cooling of affection, and suggestions as to what can be done are amongst the most compelling and insightful sections of the Kama Sutra - here, we come to understand just how much the author respects the power of feminine sexuality and its ability to rid men of their judgment, regardless of their power or wealth.

Chapter 8
Part VII – On The Means of
Attracting Others to One's Self

Throughout the *Kama Sutra*, Vatsyayana explains in detail the different techniques that could be used to attract a member of the opposite sex, or to create a pleasurable sexual experience. In this last part, Vatsyayana addresses a situation where none of these techniques have worked, and a person must resort to magical, or occult, practices.

If one cannot find love through the methods laid out in the Kama Sutra, one must resort to other methods. These include beautifying the body and using charms, aphrodisiacs, or artificial membranes. One can also beautify the eyes with makeup, enhance the texture of the skin, or drink potions to smooth the complexion. The author also explains a number of ways in which a man or woman can enhance their genitals with pastes and creams in order to make them more sexually attractive - even irresistible. (One odd suggestion is to take the remains of a kite that has fallen out of use, grind it into powder, mix it with cow dung and honey, and apply it to the body before bathing.)

The author offers a number of aphrodisiac recipes that will allow a man to stay virile (milk with sugar; licorice), vigorous (milk with sugar; the crushed testicles of a ram or a goat), or increase his stamina (vidari and kshrika fruit boiled in milk). A man can become stimulated with sugarcane roots mixed with milk, or onion powder mixed with sugar and ghee. Sexual ability can be enhanced by mixing rice with the eggs of a sparrow and then boiling the potion in milk. Other mixtures will help a man enjoy more women, preserve his life, help him recuperate from sex, or strengthen his body.

A man unable to relieve the sexual urges of a passionate woman can use his hands or even an "apadravyas" (a phallus-shaped artificial member) to stimulate orgasm. A man who is suffering sexual deficiency can be induced to orgasm by oral sex, manually, or even by inserting a finger (either the man's own or his partner's) into his anus.

Some cultures argue that a man's penis canal has to be enlarged early in pubescence. The author points specifically to Southern India, where a young male's penis is perforated with a pointed shaft to engorge the canal. A grown man can enlarge the aperture of his penis by penetrating the canal with a long wedge, provided he can stop the bleeding afterwards and sterilize the wound. Over time, he can make his penis opening larger and larger, so that it will be stronger and more powerful.

The author suggests that a man's lingam can be enlarged by the application of various pastes, by massaging the penis, or even by rubbing it with the seeds of pomegranates, cucumbers, and eggplants. The author also cites various other food combinations that can be used to alleviate different problems, such as an over-attentive man, a woman who has lost affection, a vagina that needs to be contracted or expanded, hair loss, and excessively pale lips.

This section describes various potions and ointments that could be made to make one more attractive to the person they desire. Most of these recipes created special types of adornment or decoration for the body, which would make the person more attractive. For example, if a person were to make a fine powder from the flacourtia cataphracta (Indian plum plant), and apply it to the wick of a lamp, the black pigment made from that when applied to the eyelashes, would make a person look beautiful. Or a man could take the bone of a peacock and cover it with gold, and tie it to his right hand, which would make him appear to be more attractive.

However, there are some recipes which do require magical interference of some sort. If a man took a conch shell and had it enchanted with the incantations mentioned in the Atharvana Veda (a Hindu scripture), then he would appear more attractive to others as a result of the incantations' effect.

This section does not deal only with recipes and ointments. Vatsyayana also addresses the strategy that a courtesan could use to gain a husband for her daughter when her daughter reached marriageable age. The courtesan should gather several men of a similar age to her daughter, present the daughter, and then tell the men that the one who could give her the best of a certain kind of gift would get to marry the daughter. The daughter should then be kept in seclusion until the gifts can be offered.

It is interesting to note that for courtesans' daughters, only temporary marriage was sought. A courtesan's daughter was only expected to commit to marriage for one year, and after that, she could leave the marriage. If she did choose to leave the marriage and enter into some relationship with another man, or become a courtesan herself, Vatsyayana stated that she should still return to her first husband if ever asked by him. This would apply only to returning to him for a night, not to returning the marriage itself.

After talking about the ways in which someone could make themselves more attractive to others, Vatsyayana then discusses the ointments that can be made that would allow a man to take over a woman's will so that he could have at his will. He also sets out several recipes to be used if a man wanted to increase his sexual vigor.

For ointments that would subjugate a woman to a man's will, Vatsyayana provided several options. For example, a man could cover his lingam with a mix of powders from the long pepper, the black pepper, the white thorn apple, and honey. Once the lingam was covered, if he had sex with a woman then she would be "under his spell so to speak, and she would do as he wanted with her. Covering the lingam with an ointment made from the plant emblica myrabolans (Indian gooseberry) would have the same effect. A man could also take pieces of the arris root, cover them in mango oil, and place them into a tree trunk for six months, at which point he would then make an ointment out of it to be applied to the lingam. All of these recipes would have the effect, according to Vatsyayana, of overcoming a woman's will and making her willing to do whatever the man wanted regarding sexual acts.

For recipes that could be used to increase a man's sexual vigor, there were several options as well. A drink made from mixing milk with sugar, piper chaba (a flowering vine), the root of the uchchata plant, and licorice would increase a man's sexual vigor, as would a drink made from milk, sugar, and the boiled testicle of a ram or goat.

A man could pound the seeds of the trapa bispinosa (an herb), the tuscan jasmine, the kasurika plant, and licorice, and mix it with kshirakapoli (an onion), then combine all of that with milk, sugar, and ghee and boil the concoction. After drinking the mixture, he would be able to have sex with multiple women without tiring. Or he could mix rice and sparrow eggs, boil them in milk, and add ghee and honey for the same effect.

The final book of the Kama Sutra is more concerned with tying up loose ends than with introducing core elements of the philosophy. The basic principle here involves making sure that those who cannot find sexual fulfillment and love using the other techniques in the book still have some recourse for improving their seduction and lovemaking skills. These can be divided into a few main categories - bodily improvements, sexual performance enhancements, and genital modifications.

The bodily improvements fall into line with the other aphrodisiacs mentioned in the Kama Sutra - recipes to increase stamina, vigor, ability, etc. One wonders how many of these are almost metaphorical in their nature (the potion that involves the remains of a failed kite quite obviously produces a placebo effect, if any), and whether they are directed at mothers, fathers, and other relatives who might use the placebo promise of these drinks to dupe the drinkers into truly believing in their powers.

A few of the recipes suggest that if a man or woman applies certain pastes to their genitals, there is no way a member of the opposite sex will be able to resist them. It's rather antithetical to offer miracle cures in the Kama Sutra, since so much of the book discusses the sheer amount of work necessary to perfect the art of seduction. Again, these pastes and creams can be taken as ways to build confidence in those who are uncertain of the strength of their natural powers.

The section on genital enhancement is particularly disturbing, since it appears to encourage men to use objects to pry open their penis shafts in order to increase the power of their ejaculations. This practice is not only incredibly painful, but seems likely to have a high rate of infection. The author offers a number of recipes and potions to avoid infection, but we can only assume that most readers would bypass these recommendations.

The Kama Sutra ends with this odd collection of last resorts, but we are nonetheless left with a clean arc between the books, one that centers on the theme of confidence. Indeed, the book begins with a male's responsibility to create confidence in the female, then turns to discuss a courtesan's ability to create confidence in men, and finally closes with suggestions for how both males and females can find self-confidence using a variety of remedies. This manual for sexual fulfillment, then, describes a path towards self-realization using kama, a path that will ultimately intersect with that of dharma and karma.

Charlotte Brown

Chapter 9
Translations and Modern-Day *Kama Sutra*

Due to the complex version of Sanskrit used to write the original *Kama Sutra*, for much of history, the text fell into obscurity outside of the Hindu culture, and even within it, to a large extent. In the 15th or 16th century, Kalyana Malla, an Indian poet, and author of erotic literature, wrote the *Ananga Ranga* (translated as Stage of Love, The Hindu of Art of Love, or Theatre of the Love God, to name a few). The *Ananga Ranga* drew extensively on the *Kama Sutra*. It was commissioned for a monarch of the Lodi Dynasty, by the nobleman Ladakhana. The *Ananga Ranga* eventually became much more popular than the *Kama Sutra* because it was written in a simpler, and therefore more accessible, version of Sanskrit.

Other than the *Ananga Ranga*, little studying or discussion of the *Kama Sutra* was done until the late 19th century when Sir Richard Francis Burton published an English translation. Ironically, it was the popularity of *Ananga Ranga* that led to the "rediscovery" of the *Kama Sutra* and Burton's desire to share it with the English-speaking world. Burton also translated *Ananga Ranga* in 1885.

Burton's translation remains today the most well-known English translation. It was printed in 1883 through a private printing arrangement. Sir Richard Francis Burton was the publisher, but as Burton did not read or speak Sanskrit, the majority of the work was carried out by Indian archaeologist Bhagwan Lal Indraji. Indraji worked with Indian civil servant Forster Fitzgerald Arbuthnot, who was a friend of Burton's, and a student named Shivaram Parshuram Bhide. In addition to being the publisher, Burton provided footnotes for the edition, as well as the introduction.

Burton was a fairly unique individual for his time. He was wildly interested in "foreign cultures" in a way that was appreciative and respectful of those cultures, unlike many of his fellow Brits at the time. He was fascinated by the topics of sexuality and enjoyed erotic literature, and would study the sexual practices and mores of different cultures that he visited.

The *Obscene Publications Act of 1857* greatly impeded Burton's access to erotic works, so he became involved in the private publishing of books. In the early 1880's, Burton established the Kama Shastra Society, which printed and circulated written works which were illegal to publish publicly. Burton's translation of the *Kama Sutra* was one of these publications. Another was *The Book of the Thousand Nights and a Night* (often known as *The Arabian Nights*), a ten-volume work that contained many stories of a sexual nature. One of the essays contained within that work, called *Pederasty*, was a 14,000-word discussion of homosexuality. At that time, and for a long time after, it was the longest and most thorough and outright discussion of homosexuality available.

After Burton came several translations of the *Kama Sutra*, a few of which were notable. A German-Latin text of the *Kama Sutra* was published by Richard Schmidt in 1897, likely the first translation of the *Kama Sutra* into a European language that was not English.

Indra Sinha, a British author of Indian descent, had a translation published in 1980. This version's chapter on sexual positions was circulated on the internet starting in the early 1990s, which is part of the reason why today many people believe that the *Kama Sutra* is a text about sexual positions. Often when people refer to the *Kama Sutra*, it is this chapter of Indra Sinha's translation to which they are referring.

Alain Daniélou, who was a French historian and Indologist and who studied (and converted to) Shaivite Hinduism, created a translation in 1994 called *The Complete Kama Sutra*. This translation, which was done first into French and then into English, was of note because it preserved the original document's numbered verse divisions, and it also did not have any footnotes or other notes within the text. Daniélou did include two commentaries from other writers on the *Kama Sutra*: Yashodhara's 'Jayamangala' commentary was written in Sanskrit, which was produced during the Middle Ages, and a modern commentary written in Hindi by Devadatta Shastri.

In his translation, Daniélou translated the Sanskrit words into English, although he did maintain the word "Brahmin" as it is fairly familiar to English-speaking audiences. Concerning words referring to sexual organs, he kept the words from the original rather than using the terms "lingam" and "yoni" which had frequently been used in translations of the *Kama Sutra*. His reason for keeping the original words was that he stated that "lingam" and "yoni," to a modern Hindu, were the sexual organs of the Hindu god Shiva and his wife, Parvati. He, therefore, felt that it would be irreligious or disrespectful to use those words to refer to the sexual organs of mere humans. This claim has been disputed by other academics in the area, including S.N. Balangangadhara, who is a professor at Belgium's Ghent University and a scholar of religions and cultures, with a focus on India and Hinduism.

Wendy Doniger O'Flaherty (also known as Wendy Doniger) was a scholar of the cultures, literature, and languages of the Indian subcontinent, including today's India, Bangladesh, Pakistan, Maldives, Sri Lanka, Nepal, and eastern Afghanistan. She graduated *summa cum laude* from Radcliffe College in Sanskrit and Indian Studies, obtained her M.A. from Harvard, and then received her Ph.D. from Harvard in Indian studies in 1968, and a D. Phil in Oriental Studies in 1973 from Oxford University. Dr. Doniger wrote several academic books about Indian and Hindu culture and history and also carried out a number of translations including Vātsyāyana Kāmasūtra (the *Kama Sutra*), which she worked on with Indian psychoanalyst and author Sudhir Kakar, which was published in 2003.

Dr. Kakar carried out a psychoanalytic interpretation of the text as his contribution to the translation while Dr. Doniger provided her expertise in Sanskrit. Dr. Doniger is a serious and well-respected scholar and author, who clearly felt that the *Kama Sutra* as a publication was important not only to Hindu history and culture but also to the larger society. This belief of the text's importance is demonstrated by the fact that she chose to carry out a translation of the text.

Each of these translations played a part in bringing the *Kama Sutra* into modern-day culture and introducing it to other cultures.

Kama Sutra in Modern-Day Culture

The "Kamasutra" is one of the world's oldest textbooks of erotic love and certainly the most famous. It was composed in northern India in Sanskrit, the literary language of ancient India, probably in the second century—a time when Europeans were, sexually speaking, still swinging in trees. Because of its explicitness about the intimacies of sexual passion, it can still make people today blush.

But the "Kamasutra" has long been misunderstood by many people. Very little of it, in fact, concerns the sexual act, and the bits that do may or may not surprise modern readers, depending on what sort of lives they have led. But the rest of it will surprise them, because the "Kamasutra" is, above all, a profound work of psychology.

The descriptions of sexual positions may at one time have been the most thumb-worn passages, but nowadays, when sexually explicit novels, films, videos and instruction manuals are everywhere, no one needs to read it for that. The real "Kamasutra" is about the art of living—finding a partner, maintaining power in a marriage, committing adultery, using drugs and more. It tells us that anyone can live the life of pleasure—if they have money.

A modern reader might expect the book's descriptions of sex to be familiar and the details of life in ancient India to be strange. In fact, the opposite is often true: some sexual details are strange and even repugnant while cultural matters are often surprisingly familiar.

The "Kamasutra" describes some sexual contortions that "require practice," as the text puts it mildly. These are the gymnastic positions that make people laugh, uneasily, when there is mention of book. Sexual reality may be universal—there are, after all, just so many things that you can do—but sexual fantasy seems to be highly cultural.

Did people in ancient India really make love like that? True, they did have yoga, and great yoga practitioners can make their bodies do things that most people would not think possible (or even desirable). But the extreme positions may just be the writer's free-ranging fantasies. Be advised: don't try this at home.

We are in more familiar territory with the book's psychological analysis. The acuity of the male author is still impressive today, as when he lists the sorts of married women who are likely to cheat on their husbands: a woman who has no children or whose children have died; a poor woman fond of enjoying herself; a woman who is proud of her skills and distressed by her husband's foolishness, lack of distinction or greediness; a woman whose husband travels a lot; the wife of a man who is jealous, bad-smelling, too pure, impotent, a procrastinator, unmanly, sick or old.

Equally insightful is the list of devious devices that a woman uses to make her lover leave her rather than simply kicking him out. She talks about things he does not know about. She shows no amazement but only contempt for the things he does know about. She intentionally distorts the meaning of what he says. She laughs when he has not made a joke, and when he has made a joke, she laughs about something else. She talks in public about the bad habits and vices that he cannot give up.

As these instances suggest, an aspect of the "Kamasutra" that has been lamentably overlooked is its strikingly modern attitude toward the role of women in sexual relations. One reason for this ignorance is that the text is known almost entirely through the flawed 19th-century English translation of Sir Richard Francis Burton.

Burton can be admired for the courage and determination it took to publish the work at all (it was banned in England and the U.S. until 1962), but he robs women of their voices, replacing direct quotes with reported speech rephrased by a man, thus erasing their vivid presence. For instance, the text says that, when a man strikes a woman, "She uses words like 'Stop!' or 'Let me go!' or 'Enough!' or 'Mother!'" Burton translates it like this: "She continually utters words expressive of prohibition, sufficiency or desire of liberation."

Stripped of Burton's veils, this much misunderstood text serves both as a window into the bedrooms of another culture and a mirror for our own most intimate desires.

Psychologists have noted that the *Kama Sutra* contains some very positive messages and lessons about establishing a loving and equal relationship and that sex can be used as one means of demonstrating your love for your partner. The sexual techniques and methods are all intended to improve the physical and emotional connection between men and women, thereby creating a healthy relationship that will survive long-term.

Discussions about interpreting a woman's body language, what to do when you are in a fight with your lover, how to respond to your attraction to someone, and how to woo a woman, are all relatively applicable to modern day society. For the most part, the opinions set out in the text represent a view that is quite respectful and appreciative of women and their role in the relationship, and would serve both men and women well if they were followed today.

The Kama Sutra has inspired self-help manuals, movies, books, and art. While the original Kama Sutra did not have illustrations, there have been many versions of the sex chapter of the Kama Sutra that have been produced in recent times which included beautiful and in-depth illustrations of the various sexual positions. These positions have also been expanded upon in several written works.

Charlotte Brown

Conclusion

As you have seen from reading this book, the *Kama Sutra* is a thorough and complex examination of the ancient Hindu culture and the relationships that were formed between men and women within that culture. The Kama Sutra has seven books, and begins with a description of general principles. In the beginning, Brahma, the Lord of Beings, created men and women, and laid down rules for existence that dealt with dharma, artha, and kama. Dharma is the fulfillment of one's duty during one's life on earth, artha is the accumulation of material wealth, and kama refers to the pleasurable experience of the five senses. While many tend to discount the importance of kama, it is the goal of the Kama Sutra to guide those in the experience of sexual pleasure and the fulfillment of love. Dharma is more important than artha, and artha is more important than kama, and yet kama is often applied improperly, leading to an undue focus on it in relation to dharma and artha. The Kama Sutra says that kama should be studied not only by men, but also by women. Indeed, women should have a full knowledge of the arts and sciences, and especially those arts that are complimentary to the Kama Sutra. A full list of arts suitable for women are listed, including intellectual pastimes, useful athletics, magic, sorcery, and aphrodisiacs.

Men are divided into three classes, depending on the size of their lingam (or phallus): hare; bull; or horse. Women, meanwhile, are divided into categories based on the size of their yoni (or genitalia): deer; mare; or elephant. In order to produce an equal union, the size of a man's lingam should match that of his partner's yoni. Once a union is equal, a man and woman can begin practicing the Chatus-Shasti, or the 64 forms of sexual union, in an effort to achieve true fulfillment of pleasure. The first position is the Alinganam, or the embrace - and the final position is Adhoratam, or anal congress. The author says that which of the Chatus-Shasti is performed depends on "the liking of each individual, the generation of love, friendship, and the respect accorded to the woman."

The third book discusses betrothal and marriage. In order to bring about a marriage a man must take a kanya, or virgin maid, and both families should be called upon to assist in the matter. In addition, it should be verified with the astrologers that the union is auspicious. For the first three days after marriage, the new husband and wife should abstain from sexual pleasures. The male should build the female's confidence and gradually introduce her to the possibilities of sexual pleasure. Over the course of ten days, the man should continue to build her confidence until she is fully receptive and unafraid of sexual connection. This building of confidence is crucial, as a man must recognize the signs that indicate that a girl is not only ready for sexual connection, but that her affection has reached a sufficient point to allow him to assert his natural dominance over her.

The fourth book explains the role of the wife. There are four types of love: love that emerges by habit; love by imagination; mutual love as imagined by both parties; and love that is not defined as such by the parties, but is rather known to the outside world. A wife's main role is to keep the house functional - clean, with food on the table, well-maintained, and self-sufficient. Meals are a crucial part of a woman's duties and she should make sure to consider what her husband likes and dislikes and what things are good for him. If a wife shows folly or ill-temper, is disliked by her husband, cannot bear children, or continually births girls, the man is free to take a second wife, whom the first wife must care for like a daughter.

Book five explores the inherent nature of men and women, explaining that women tend to fall in love much harder, but not for any particular purpose. In other words, a woman will naturally shrink from a man because of the force of her love, and needs to be conquered and persistently approached in order to trust the man who would warrant such strong feelings. Men, on the other hand, tend to get indifferent when faced with rejection, and so the Kama Sutra instructs men to see it as a natural consequence of innate female resistance; it is the most persistent and devoted men who gain their true loves. The author also lays out a series of strategies a man can use to woo a female, including using friends, dootis (or go-betweens), and boastful behavior in front of the girl to show how powerful, special, or desirable he is to her. Most importantly, both the male and female must be attentive to the other's specific behavior in order to see how to manipulate, and likely modify their seduction. A king, however, is exempt from all of this, and is allowed to have as many wives as he wants without having to enter the whole process of seduction. If he likes a women, he can simply have her kidnapped and imprisoned on false causes in order to add her to his royal court.

The sixth book discusses the vaishika, or the courtesan. The Kama Sutra says that the courtesan is necessary in order to ensure that men have companions in times of need, or to build their confidence before they begin pursuing a wife. Some women are born courtesans, depending on their caste and status of birth, and there is no stigma to being a courtesan, as long as one behaves with decency and propriety. A courtesan must be careful to attract desirable patrons and paramours, as well as suitable protectors, to ensure her safety - but her first priority is making sure she chooses patrons who can be depended upon for monetary support. Getting money by all means is an art that has to be developed by a courtesan through manipulation and artifice, which includes flattery, lies, and elaborate game-playing. In the end, once a vaishika sees that a man is beginning to lose interest in her, she must quickly move on and end the relationship before he does so himself.

The final book is a short exploration of sexual lore, and offers a number of strategies for men and women to beautify the body in order to ensure that they are more sexually attractive. These include pastes, ointments, and oils for the body, including the genitalia. Also included are recipes for home remedies that can cure various sexual deficiencies like lack of stamina, impotence, lack of sexual ability, etc. In conclusion, the author states that an intelligent and prudent person, attending to dharma and artha and attending to kama also, without becoming the slave of his passions, obtains success in everything that he may undertake.

While the author Vatsyayana wrote the *Kama Sutra* to reflect the religious and moral expectations of that culture, there are certainly many lessons that can be taken from the text and applied to relationships of today.

This application of the *Kama Sutra* to modern-day culture does not apply only to sexual acts, but also to how men and women should value each other and seek to please each other both sexually and in other aspects of the relationship. In the last century, in particular, the popular focus on the *Kama Sutra* has been on the sexual components of the text, yet there is much more to be learned from Vatsyayana's work.

Thank you for reading this book. I hope that you enjoyed it.

Charlotte Brown